Learn French
Like a Native
for Beginners

COLLECTION

Learning French in Your Car Has Never Been Easier! Have Fun with Crazy Vocabulary, Daily Used Phrases, Exercises & Correct Pronunciations

www.LearnLikeNatives.com

© **Copyright 2021 By Learn Like A Native**

ALL RIGHTS RESERVED

No part of this book may be reproduced, stored in a retrieval system, or transmitted in any form or by any means, without the prior written permission of the publisher.

Table of Contents

INTRODUCTION 1

CHAPTER 1 – THE FIRST IMPRESSION IS VERY IMPORTANT 10

CHAPTER 2 – ARE WE RELATED? 20

CHAPTER 3 – WHAT DAY IS IT? 29

CHAPTER 4 – THERE IS NO GIFT LIKE THE PRESENT 41

CHAPTER 5 – HAVE A LOOK AROUND 53

CHAPTER 6 – HOW FAR CAN YOU COUNT? 61

CHAPTER 7 – WHAT DID YOU WANT TO BE WHEN YOU GREW UP?
.... 68

CHAPTER 8 – WHERE ARE WE GOING? 79

CHAPTER 9 – SURVIVAL 101 85

CHAPTER 10 – WHAT IS THE COLOR OF THE SKY? 91

CHAPTER 11 – SO MUCH TO DO, SO MUCH TO SEE 97

CHAPTER 12 : I AM A BIT HUNGRY 107

CONCLUSION 118

.... 121

CHAPTER 1 – DREAMING OF THE SOUTH 128

CHAPTER 2 – NOT ONLY BIRDS CAN FLY 146

CHAPTER 3 – LOOKING FOR A RIDE? 155

CHAPTER 4 – I FIND MY HAPPINESS WHERE THE SUN SHINES.... 165

CHAPTER 5 – I HAVE SO MANY STORIES TO TELL YOU 174

CHAPTER 6 – SO MANY ROADS AND SO MANY PLACES.............. 195

CHAPTER 7 – EAT, TRAVEL, LOVE 203

CHAPTER 8 – SICK & ABROAD! 210

CHAPTER 9 – LEARN THE ROPES................................. 216

CHAPTER 10 – BRING, LEARN & LEAD........................... 224

CHAPTER 11 – NEW JOB, NEW LIFE 236

CHAPTER 12 – BRINGING HOME THE BACON 244

CONCLUSION 252

.... 254

Learn French Like a Native for Beginners - Level 1

Learning French in Your Car Has Never Been Easier! Have Fun with Crazy Vocabulary, Daily Used Phrases, Exercises & Correct Pronunciations

www.LearnLikeNatives.com

Introduction

Benefits of Learning French

It is easy to stick with your native tongue. As an English speaker, you may feel that you have a considerable advantage. But are you not fascinated by other languages? By different cultures? Do you not find them captivating?

Let's say you are going to your holiday destination (maybe France, or even just a French-speaking country). Did you think of everything? First aid kit, papers, and documents? Very good, but what about your foreign language skills? Have you ever thought about how you will express yourself? Unfortunately, many travelers neglect this topic and believe that, with English, you can get anywhere. Some also assume you can communicate well with your hands and feet. The question you should ask yourself, though, is:

What do I expect from my journey, and which goals do I have (besides just relaxing, of course)?

To give you a little motivation, here are five advantages of being able to express yourself in the language of the country you are in:

- You get to know the locals much more authentically
- You understand the culture and attitude of people much better
- You can negotiate more effectively
- You do not waste valuable time, because you can communicate faster
- You feel safer

Just to keep it short, you do not have to learn a foreign language to perfection.

A Bit of History About This Beautiful Language...

French is a poetic language. There's something about the way the string of words sounds like. It is as if it is meant to woo a lover.

You may then be surprised to discover that French was actually derived from Vulgar Latin, the kind spoken by Roman soldiers. By 200 BC, this form of Latin became more popular and widespread throughout the Empire. Vulgar Latin gave birth to French and other romantic languages we know today - Italian, Spanish, Romanian, and Portuguese.

The Perfect Method

I'm sure you've been told there's no right or wrong way to learn a language. Well, that can't be right, because it's wrong! The truth is, most people don't lack in motivation, drive, excitement, determination, or even talent. More than anything, people lack the correct method.

I've been learning and teaching languages my whole life, and I've realized that the number one reason why people get stuck learning any language is simple. It's not because they are lazy, it's not because they don't have time, it's because they are bored!

You could go to the best schools and have the best teachers in the world, but if you're bored in your Spanish class, you're unlikely to get anywhere. Starting from scratch and ingesting new knowledge can be a daunting thing as it is. So, if you're not fully engaged, learning a new language will be a long road.

Think about it. You've been a child before. Did you learn grammar before you knew how to speak? Of course not! So why do that now? In my opinion, that's where most language methods fail. They get caught up in all the specific rules and formal details, before worrying about whether or not their students understand what's going on. What's the point in knowing irregular verbs, if you can't even order food at the restaurant! My point being, unless you're planning to write a Ph.D. in French, the most important thing for you is to be able to speak with other people.

That's where Learn Like A Native comes in!

With approximately 120 million people who speak and study French as a non-native language, there's plenty of opinions as to what the best way to learn is.

That's why I based my method on modern expert research. The latest studies show that the most efficient way to learn languages – and French in particular – is by learning vocabulary and grammar in conversation.

Using this method, I'll teach you how to apply formal knowledge in a real-life environment, through practical and relatable materials. With short and fun lessons, you'll stay engaged every step of the way, helping you retain vocabulary much more efficiently.

The audiobook version is narrated by a French native speaker who will get you comfortable with the sounds of the language. You'll take an active part in the learning process and be required to speak, repeat, and exercise new sounds as they come up throughout the lessons. If you have any trouble, the textbook will help you with written sounds so you can visualize letters and the sound they relate to.

You'll feel like you're in a French class. But one you can take everywhere! With only 20 to 30 minutes per lesson, you can focus on each topic independently without any stress. Squeeze them into your schedule, sitting in your car or waiting for the Bus, and enjoy the flexibility of going through each step at your own pace. No one is watching you, of course, but I trust you'll do the work!

Learning a new language is a complex and rich experience. After you are done with this book, you will be ready (or more prepared) to travel, immerse yourself in French-speaking cultures, read fiction and newspapers in French, watch films, eat French foods, learn recipes, make French-speaking friends and, most importantly, enjoy yourself!

This book is inspiring and vibrant to read and/or listen to, motivating you to speak and embrace the French language, no matter how new you are to it. Before you know it, you'll find yourself having a full-blown conversation in French and wonder how you got there!

Are you ready? Okay, then we can start. Whichever language level you achieve depends entirely on you.

www.LearnLikeNatives.com

FREE BOOK!

Get the *FREE BOOK* that reveals the secrets path to learn any language fast, and without leaving your country.

Discover:

- The **language 5 golden rules** to master languages at will

- Proven **mind training techniques** to revolutionize your learning

- A complete step-by-step guide to **conquering any language**

www.LearnLikeNatives.com

www.LearnLikeNatives.com

Chapter 1 – The first impression is very important

Everyone knows the old saying "you only get one chance to make a first impression."

Therefore, it's no surprise that one of the first things every child learns is to say hello and introduce themselves. Even J.K. Rowling, the famous author of that young wizard's adventures, said "A good first impression can work wonders", and I completely agree.

Just a simple "Hello" can make all the difference in a conversation. That's exactly the reason why we will begin this exciting adventure, learning greetings in French. You will learn how to introduce yourself and greet people at different times of the day, among other useful things.

We will start with the most popular greetings. There are several ways of greeting people in French, depending on who you are addressing and whether you want to be formal or not.

Ready to start? I really hope you are as excited as I am!

So, let's start with the most common ways to greet someone in French:

Hello.	Bonjour/Salut

Bon-joor – Sah-luh

The word "Bonjour" is probably one of the most popular French words and is now used as a friendly salutation around the world.

Salut, which is more informal, is also used quite often, but applies more to people you know personally, such as friends and family.

Good morning.	Bonjour

Translated literally, "Bonjour" means "good day". It is also used as a greeting upon waking up. You can use it in the morning and afternoon.

Contrary to English, the greetings don't change depending on the time of the day. As such, in the afternoon, you also say "Bonjour".

As the afternoon sets in, you should say "Good evening".

Good evening.	Bonsoir

Bon-swar

You can use this greeting on both formal and informal occasions. It is used both for when you are arriving and leaving a place.

Finally, at bedtime, you will say:

| Good night. | Bonne nuit |

Boh-nuh nu-ee

Remember! You should use "Bonne nuit" only when you are saying goodbye late at night. It is also used to wish sweet dreams.

Last one. When departing, you say:

| Goodbye. | Au revoir / Ciao |

Au revoir – Tchah-oh

You should remember that, depending on whether you are greeting a friend or a stranger, you would use a different salutation.

For example, when leaving a restaurant (or in any other formal occasion), you will say "Au revoir" if you want to sound polite. Although, you can use "Ciao" if you are saying goodbye to some old friends or to someone you know well (informal occasion).

Farewell.	Adieu
Farewell. I love you.	**Adieu**. Je t'aime

Ah-dee-euh

"Adieu" is used as a final salutation when you are pretty sure you are not going to see someone ever again. It's a phrase very rich in drama, sadness, or irony.

There is also a more informal version of "Au revoir"

See you later.	A plus tard.
Great! **See you later.**	Parfait! **À plus tard.**

Ah-plu-tar

How is your pronunciation? Hope you are starting to make progress.

See you in a few.	À tout à l'heure
Ok! **See you in a few.**	Okl! **À tout à l'heure.**

A-toot-a-leur

When greeting, you may also want to ask how someone is doing.

How are you?	Comment ça va? / ça va?

Ko-man-sah-vah

Asking "Comment ça va?" is a really good way to start a friendly conversation. It is an informal greeting and can also be used between people you are familiar with to ask about their health or mood. You can also simply say: ça va? There is no big difference between the two. Here's the literal translation of both expressions:

-Comment ça va? "How are you doing?"
-ça va? Are you alright/Are you okay?

How can I help you?	Comment je peux t'aider?

Koh-man-guh-puh-teh-deh

At this point, you have probably figured out the connection between two words: "how" and "comment", and you know how important the word "how" is in any language.

Let's see another sentence that uses the word "Comment":

| What is your name? | Comment tu t'appelles? |

Ko-man-tah-pel-tu

To say what your name is in French you use:

| My name is | Je m'appelle |
| **My name is** John. | **Je m'appelle** John. |

Juh-ma-pell

| I am | Je suis |
| **I am** new around here. | **Je suis** nouveau ici. |

Juh-suee

| Thanks/Thank you. | Merci |

Mer-see

"Merci" is used to say both "thanks" or "thank you". However, if you wish to show more gratitude, you could say "Thanks a lot" which translates to "Merci beaucoup".

Mer-see-bo-koo

| I am sorry. | Je suis désolé. |

Juh-suee-dé-zo-lé

| Nice to see you again. | Ravi de te revoir. |

Ra-vee-duh-tuh-ruh-vwar

Was it too hard? Don't worry. Greetings are basic phrases you will need to memorize, but I promise that following sentences will be shorter and easier to remember.

| What is new? | Quoi de neuf? |

Kwa-duh-neuf

Another sentence with similar meaning is "Qu'est-ce que tu racontes?" What do you say?

Ke-suh-kuh-tu-ra-ko-ntuh

| How are you doing? | Comment vas-tu? Comment ça va? |

Ko-man-va-tu

As you might know, "Ok" is an English expression. Nevertheless, it's universally used worldwide, even among French speakers. You should be aware, however, that there is a French equivalent:

Ok.	D'accord

Da-kor

How is it going? Is it easy? Or maybe you need to practice a little bit more. Practice is the key to mastery. Anyway, before we move to another topic, let's take a look at a short conversation that uses some of the words we have just learned.

You'll now listen to a short dialog between John and a Vendor.

You'll listen to the sentences, first in English and then in French.

Vendor   *Good morning!*

(Vendeur):   Bonjour

John: *Good morning to you, too.*

	Bonjour à vous.
Vendor:	*How can I help you?*
	Comment puis-je vous aider?
John:	*I am here to pick up a cake.*
	Je suis ici pour récupérer un gâteau.
Vendor:	*Sure. What is your name?*
	Bien-sûr. Quel est votre nom?
John:	*My name is John Hill.*
	Je m'appelle John Hill.
Vendor:	*Oh, I am sorry. Your bday cake is not ready yet.*
	Oh, je suis désolé. Votre gâteau d'anniversaire n'est pas encore prêt.
John:	*Ok. When can I come pick it up?*
	D'accord. Quand est-ce que je peux venir le récuperer?
Vendor:	*It will be ready in one hour.*

	Ce sera prêt dans une heure.
John:	*Great. I will run some errands and come back.*
	Super. Je vais faire quelques courses et je reviens.
Vendor:	*Thanks for understanding. See you in a few.*
	Merci de votre compréhension. A tout à l'heure.
John:	*Sure. See you later!*
	Bien-sûr. A plus tard!

I hope John is not getting low blood sugar, because he will have to wait for a while. In the meantime, shall we go and learn some new words and phrases that relate to family and relatives? This could be really handy if you are going to celebrate your birthday!

Chapter 2 – Are we related?

I am sure your family would be pleased to tell you the story of your first word.

Language acquisition starts with receptive language, the understanding of sounds and words of the world around us. There is a good chance that either "mum" or "dad" (or a variable of these) was the first word you learned.

Dad	Papa
My **dad** went out to get more ice.	Mon **papa** est sorti chercher plus de glace.

Pah-pah

In the French language, usually the last syllable of each rhythmic group inside the sentence is pronounced at a higher pitch than the rest of the sentence. Here, we'll put the accent on the last « a ». **Pah-pah**

Mom	Maman
My **mom** is there, by the corner.	Ma **maman** est là-bas, vers le coin.

Mah-man

Son	Fils
My **son** used to play tennis.	Mon **fils** jouait au tennis avant.

Fiss

Daugther	Fille
My daughter likes to dance.	Ma **fille** aime danser.

Fee-yuh

Unlike English, French nouns have a gender *(genre)*:

They can be masculine *(masculin)* or feminine *(féminin)*. There are different ways to find out a noun's gender: we can look in the dictionary and check for the abbreviations *m.* *(masculine)* or *f.* *(feminine)*; we can check the noun's ending, which generally gives an indication whether the noun is masculine or feminine; or we can look at the noun's article.

Nouns with the article *le* or *un* are masculine, and nouns with *la* or *une* are feminine. You should always learn nouns together with their articles to be sure of their gender.

Notice the difference between "mon" and "ma", both meaning "my".

In fact, "mon" is used for "my son", which is a masculine word. For "my daughter", which is a feminine word, we'll use "ma".

Brother	Frère
This is my **brother** Alex.	Voici mon **frère** Alex.

Freh-ruh

Sister	Soeur
She is my **sister** Coreen.	Elle, c'est **ma soeur** Coreen.

Suhr

Uncle	Oncle
I have two **uncles**.	J'ai deux **oncles.**

On-k-luh

| Aunt | Tante |

My **aunt** has two kids.	Ma **tante** a deux enfants.

Tan-tuh

- Most French nouns also form their plural by adding an **-s** to their singular form. But remember, this **-s** is always silent

Cousin	Cousin
My cousin lives far from here	Mon **cousin** vit loin d'ici.

Koo-zen

This one's easy to remember! It's the same word with a different pronounciation.

Grandfather	Grand-père
My **grandpa** picks up mangoes every day.	Mon **grand-père** cueille des mangues tous les jours.

Gran-peh-ruh

Grandmother	Grand-mère

My **grandma** loved knitting.	Ma **grand-mère** adorait tricoter.

Gran-peh-ruh

How is it going so far? Don't you worry, we just need to meet few more people, and then we can take a short break.

Siblings	Frères/Soeurs
I have three **siblings**.	J'ai trois **frères/soeurs**.

Freh-ruh/ Su-uhr

Parents	Parents
I love my **parents**.	J'aime mes **parents**.

Pah-ran

Family	Famille
My **family** is big.	J'ai une grande **famille**.

Fah-meey

Neighbor	Voisin
Dan is a great **neighbor**.	Dan est un **voisin** super.

Vwa-zen

www.LearnLikeNatives.com

Are you ready to use the words you just learned? Great!

Let's listen to a short conversation.

You'll listen to the sentences, first in English and then in French.

Allyson: *Happy birthday!*

Joyeux anniversaire!

Kelly: *Hello! Thanks a lot! I am happy that you came.*

Salut! Merci beaucoup! Je suis contente que tu sois venue.

Allyson: *I am happy that you invited me.*

Je suis contente que tu m'aies invitée

Kelly: *Sure. Let me show you who everyone is.*

	Bien-sûr. Laisse moi te montrer qui est qui.

Allyson: *Great!*

Super!

Kelly: *That girl is my sister, and my cousin John is sitting next to her.*

Cette fille est ma soeur, et mon cousin John est assis à côté d'elle.

Allyson: *Yeah. Next to them is your brother Mark, right?*

Oui. A côté d'eux c'est ton frère Mark, c'est ça?

Kelly: *Perfect! Yes. He picks me up sometimes.*

Parfait! Oui. Il vient me chercher parfois.

Allyson: *I remember.*

Je me souviens.

Kelly: *Good. By that other corner are grandma, grandpa and uncle Ed.*

Bien. Vers là-bas. Il y a ma grand-mère, mon grand-père et mon oncle Ed.

Allyson: *Your grandma looks so young!*

Ta grand-mère a l'air tellement jeune!

Kelly: *Yes. I hope I have the same luck.*

Oui. J'espère que j'aurais la même chance.

Allyson: *Don't we all?*

On l'espère tous, non?

Kelly: *Let's see... who's missing? Oh, well. Dad is outside,*

> *with the neighbors and the rest of the family.*
>
> Voyons voir… Qui manque? Ah, oui. Mon père est dehors avec les voisins et le reste de la famille.

Allyson: *Great! I can't wait to meet them.*

Super! J'ai hâte de les rencontrer.

So, what do you think? Learning a new language is about listening to things over and over again and repeating many times. My advice is to always say the words out loud when practicing, so you should be able to see significant improvement moving on the next chapters.

www.LearnLikeNatives.com

Chapter 3 – What day is it?

Learn how to measure and tell the time is hugely important. In many cultures, punctuality is extremely important and viewed as a form of respect, and I personally think it is a great sign of courtesy. Of course, you will also learn the days of the week and months, so you can make plans. Another thing you may want to know when traveling abroad is what season is it, to know how to dress accordingly.

Second	Seconde
One minute has sixty **seconds**.	Une minute équivaut à soixante **secondes**.

Seh-gon-duh

Minute	Minute
One hour has sixty **minutes**.	Une heure équivaut à soixante **minutes**.

Mee-nu-tuh

Hour	Heure

There are twenty-four **hours** in a day.	Il y a vingt-quatre **heures** dans une journée.

Eu-ruh

Great, let's carry on.

Day	Jour
January has thirty-one **days**.	Il y a trente-et-un **jours** en Janvier.

Joor

Week	Semaine
We have one **week** to finish.	Nous avons une **semaine** pour terminer.

Suh-main-uh

Month	Mois
We will be there next **month**.	Nous serons là le **mois** prochain.

Mwah

Year	Année

| One more birthday, one more **year**. | Un anniversaire de plus, une **année** de plus. |

Ah-neh

Decade	Décennie
This **decade** is going to end soon.	Cette **décennie** va bientôt se terminer.

Deh-seh-nee

Century	Siècle
This is the discovery of the **century**.	C'est la découverte du **siècle**.

See-eh-kluh

Morning	Matin
The meeting was this **morning**.	La réunion était ce **matin**.

Mah-ten

Afternoon	Après-midi
Will you be there in the **afternoon**?	Tu seras là cet **après-midi**?

Ah-preh-mee-dee

Night	Nuit
The Moon comes out at **night**.	La lune sort la **nuit.**

Nu-ee

Spring	Printemps
Everything flowers in **spring**.	Tout fleurit au **printemps**.

Pren-tam

Summer	Eté
We had a fun **summer**.	Nous avons eu un **été** divertissent.

Eh-teh

Autumn	Automne
Look at the first **autumn** leaf.	Regardes la première feuille d'**automne**.

Oh-to-nuh

Winter	Hiver

| **W**i**nter** is here. | l'**hiver** est arrivé. |

Ee-ver

| January | Janvier |
| **January** is the first month of the year. | **Janvier** est le premier mois de l'année. |

Jan-vee-eh

| February | Février |
| That tree flowers in **February**. | Cet arbre fleurit en **Février**. |

Feh-vree-eh

| March | Mars |
| **March** is a good month for harvesting. | **Mars** est un bon mois pour la récolte. |

Mars

| April | Avril |
| We stop activities in **April**. | Nous arrêtons les activités en **Avril**. |

Ah-vreel

Have you noticed how most of the names of the months are similar between English and French? That's a relief, isn't it?

May	Mai
May is going to be a great month.	**Mai** va être un mois super.

Meh

June	Juin
The break starts in **June**.	Les vacances commencent en **Juin**.

Ju-ein

July	Juillet
July is a hot month in France.	**Juillet** est un mois chaud en France.

Ju-ee-yeh

August	Août
This **August** will be rainy.	Ce mois d'**Août** sera pluvieux.

Ah-oo-t

September	Septembre
Next semester starts in **September**.	Le prochain semestre commence en **Septembre**.

Sep-ten-bruh

October	Octobre
My birthday is in **October**.	Mon anniversaire est en **Octobre**.

Ok-to-bruh

November	Novembre
We celebrated Halloween all **November**.	Nous avons célébré Halloween tout le mois de **Novembre**.

Noh-vem-bruh

December	Décembre
Year ends in **December**.	L'année se termine en **Décembre**.

Deh-cem-bruh

Monday	Lundi

| Today is **Monday**. | Aujourdhui, c'est **Lundì**. |

Leun-dee

| Tuesday | Mardi |
| I have an appointment for next **Tuesday**. | J'ai un rendez-vous pour **Mardì** prochain. |

Mar-dee

| Wednesday | Mercredi |
| **Wednesday** is not a good day for me. | **Mercredi** n'est pas un bon jour pour moi. |

Mer-kruh-dee

| Thursday | Jeudi |
| I'll see you next **Thursday**. | Je vous verrai **jeudi** prochain. |

Juh-dee

| Friday | Vendredi |
| The party is next **Friday**. | La fête est **Vendredi** prochain. |

Ven-druh-dee

Saturday	Samedi
I play every **Saturday**.	Je joue tous les **Samedis**.

Sah-muh-dee

Sunday	Dimanche
We can have lunch this **Sunday**.	Nous pouvons déjeuner ensemble ce **Dimanche**.

dDee-man-shuh

How is it going? Are you ready for a short dialogue?

Ally: *So, what are your plans for next year?*

Alors, quels sont tes plans pour l'année prochaine?

Juan: *I honestly don't know what will happen after winter.*

Sincèrement, je ne sais pas ce qui va se passer après l'hiver.

Ally: *Will you at least come back in February? The spring is lovely here.*

Tu pourras au moins revenir en Février? Le printemps est superbe ici.

Juan: *If I don't, I promise I will be back to celebrate summer, in July.*

Si je ne reviens pas, je promets que je serais là en Juillet, pour célébrer l'été.

Ally: *Everyone loves summer. I love autumn.*

Tout le monde adore l'été. Moi j'adore l'automne.

Juan: *Why?*

Pourquoi?

Ally: *Leaves change colors and I love the weather between September and November.*

Les feuilles changent de couleur et j'adore le climat entre Septembre et Novembre.

Juan: Two weeks ago you didn't love in it that much.

Il y a deux semaines tu n'aimais pas tellement ça.

Ally: Are you talking of that rainy Wednesday? I hated that.

Tu parles de ce mercredi pluvieux? J'ai détésté.

Juan: Yeah. As if it was not enough with those boring Mondays.

Oui. Comme si ces lundi ennuyants n'étaient pas assez.

Ally: Oh, sure. I don't like Mondays. I love Fridays.

C'est sur. Je n'aime pas les lundis. J'adore les vendredis.

Juan: Like everyone. But I like Saturdays better.

Comme tout le monde. Mais je préfère les samedis.

Ally: Yes. Especially the ones in Spring, when you take your boat for a ride.

Oui. Surtout au printemps. Quand tu peux prendre ton bâteau pour faire un tour.

Juan: You remember it. Good.

Tu t'en souviens. Super.

It is not as hard as you thought, right? There is a lot to remember, but sometimes it's easier if you find the similarities between English and French, as some in the names of the months. And let us repeat, practice makes perfect.

Now has come the time to learn some important verbs and how to conjugate them.

Chapter 4 – There is no gift like the Present

Just as in any other language, in French, verbs are an important part of everyday speaking. When studying a foreign language, the present is the first tense you learn as this allows you to form simple sentences. It is used to describe something that is happening right now or a state of being. Using the present tense, you will be able to speak about your desires, interests and plans.

First of all, in French, verb conjugation is done by changing the ending of the verb. Verbs are divided into 3 different categories of verbs, called "conjugations" – as in English. Each one is characterized by a specific ending in its infinitive form:

- First conjugation: Verbs ending in -ER (like aimer)
- Second conjugation: Verbs ending in -IR (like dormir)
- Third conjugation: Verbs ending in -RE (like croire)

In this chapter, I will teach you how to conjugate the regular verbs.

Hopefully, with a bit of practice, you will realize that French verb conjugation is actually much easier than it seems.

So, let's get started. There is no time like the present!

To love	Aimer	Root	Termination
I love	J'aime	Aim-	ER changes for "e"
You love	Tu aimes		ER changes for "es"
He/She loves	Il/Elle aime		ER changes for "e"
We love	Nous aimons		ER changes for "ons"
You love	Vous aimez		ER changes for "ez"
They love	Ils/Elles aiment		ER changes for "ent"

The root of all regular verbs never changes. As you can see, the root is the part preceding the infinitive ending. So, for example, in "Aimer" the root is "Aim-". As we said, the root always remains the same and different endings are added to denote the person, number or tense. Let's look at some examples.

I love the rain.	J'aime la pluie.
She loves the music.	Elle aime la musique.
You love movies.	Tu aimes les films.
They love to play music.	Ils aiment jouer de la musique.

Great! Here is a tip: using the above table you will be able to conjugate every other regular verb that ends in "-ER", all you will have to do is add to the root the relevant ending, as we just did. Clearly, the same logic applies to verb of the second and third conjugation (-IR and -RE). That's good to know, right?

Here are a few more examples. For the verb "to sing" - "chanter", you can separate the root "Chant-", and all you will need to do is to add the correct ending, as previously explained. The root of the verb "to sleep" – "dormir" is "dor-", and of the verb "to sell" - "vendre", the root is "Vend-".

Let's exercise with a fundamental verb: finir. In this case, the root is "Fin-".

To finish	Finir	Root	Termination
I finish	Je finis	Fini-	Ir changes for "s"
You finish	Tu finis		Ir changes for "s"
He/She finishes	Il/Elle finit		Ir changes for "t"
We finish	Nous finissons		Ir changes for "ons"
You finish	Vous finissez		Ir changes for "ez"

| They finish | Ils/Elles finissent | | Ir changes for "ent" |

So, anyhow, what do you like to do in your free time? What

I finish work at 5pm.	Je finis de travailler à 17h.
She finishes school early today.	Elle finit l'école tôt aujourd'hui.
He finishes building his house.	Il finit de construire sa maison.
They finish their meal.	Ils finissent leur repas.

are your interests? What are you passionate about? Come on, think about this for a moment. Verbs are important to discuss all of these things.

To believe	**Croire**	**Root**	**Termination**
I believe	Je crois	Cro-	RE changes for "is"

You believe	Tu crois		RE changes for "is"
He/She believes	Il/Elle croit		RE changes for "it"
We believe	Nous croyons		RE changes for "yons"
You believe	Vous croyez		RE changes for "yez"
They believe	Ils croient		RE changes for "ient"

Note that even though they are written differently, the 1st, 2nd, 3rd singular person, as well as the 3rd plural person, are pronounced the same. This applies to all French verbs. Isn't that amazing?

You believe in loyalty.	Tu crois en la loyauté.
He believes in what he can touch.	Il croit en ce qu'il peut toucher.

| You believe in yourselves. | Vous croyez en vous-même. |
| They believe in you. | Ils croient en toi. |

The root of the verb "Croire" is "Cro-".

So, what have you learned, and what do you have faith in? Repeat with me: "Je crois….". Eventually, you will be able to better express yourself in French, but –in the meantime- "Je crois" is good enough.

Now let's look at the present of the auxiliary verb "to be" – "être". This verb is one of the most versatile and you will use it a lot in French, to introduce yourself, find out more about something or someone, describe places and things, etc. It is an auxiliary verb and its purpose is to help other verbs conjugate in compound tenses. In other words, it helps to create more complex sentences and tenses.

To be	**Être**
I am	Je suis
You are	Tu es

He/She/It is	Il/Elle est
We are	Nous sommes
You are	Vous êtes
They are	Ils sont

Alongside the verb "to be", "to have" – "avoir" – is the second most important verb in the French language. It is an auxiliary and irregular verb. It allows you to express numerous things: possessing something (literally or in a figurative way), communicate, express your needs and desires, etc.

To have	**Avoir**
I have	J'ai
You have	Tu as
He/She has	Il/Elle a
We have	Nous avons
You have	Vous avez

| They have | Ils ont |

I have a meeting at nine.	J'ai une reunion à neuf heures.
He has a television at home.	Il a une television à la maison.
We have a plan.	Nous avons un plan.
They have a place by the lake.	Ils ont une propriété près du lac.

Now let's see how the « présent progressif » - the present progressive – can help us.

The « présent progressif » could be compared to the present continuous in English. It forms with the verb to be in the present and the expression « en train de » + verb to infinitive.

The expression *être en train de* + infinitive verb is used to emphasize actions in progress, similar to the present progressive tense in English. These constructions take a conjugated form of the verb *être* (in the present) + *en train de* + inifinitive verb.

www.LearnLikeNatives.com

Unlike the simple present tense, which is sometimes used for actions in progress, *être en train de* never describes a regular or habitual action.

Examples:

What are you doing ? I'm working.	Tu fais quoi ? Je suis en train de travailler.
Have you finished writing the letter ? We are finishing.	Tu as fini d'écrire la lettre ? Nous sommes en train de finir.
Did he go to the grocery store? He is shopping right now.	Est-il allé au supermarché? Il fait les courses maintenant.
They are taking a test in classroom A.	Ils sont entrain de passer une évaluation dans la salle A.

Are you looking forward to putting this into practice?

Emma: *Hi. I am Emma.*

   Salut. Je suis Emma.

www.LearnLikeNatives.com

David: *Nice to meet you. I am David.*

Enchanté. Je suis David.

Emma: *Tell me, David. What do you like to do?*

Dis moi, David. Qu'est-ce que tu aimes faire?

David: *I enjoy sailing on weekends.*

J'aime faire de la voile les weekends.

Emma: *Do you have a boat?*

Tu as un bâteau?

David: *Yes, I do. And what do you like to do?*

Oui, j'en ai un. Et qu'est-ce que tu aimes faire?

Emma: *I have a dancing academy. I love to teach.*

J'ai un club de dance. J'adore enseigner.

David: *Really? I have a niece. She loves to dance.*

Vraiment? J'ai une niece qui adore danser.

Emma: *Great! How old is she?*

Super! Elle a quel âge?

David: *She is 6 years old. Turns 7 in two weeks.*

Elle a 6 ans. Elle aura 7 ans dans deux semaines.

Emma: *I teach from 7. Maybe you could bring her. I am currently working on a ballet choreography.*

J'enseigne à partir de 7 ans. Peut-être que tu pourrais l'amener. Je suis en train de travailler sur une chorégraphie de ballet.

David: *Awesome. I am sure she will love it.*

Génial. Je suis sûr qu'elle va adorer.

As you can see, is very important to know how to conjugate the Present simple. Carry on with the practice until you achieve a better understanding.

Chapter 5 – Have a look around

N ow, have a look around the room and tell me what you see. What is in the room? For instance, I usually keep a bottle of water on my desk, and I always carry my mobile phone and wallet. In this chapter, we will learn the names of a few things that you will probably have in your house.

Clock	Horloge
My **clock** says it is late.	Mon **horloge** indique qu'il est tard.

Or-loh-guh

Remember what we said at the beginning about punctuality? You will need a "horloge" to always be right on time.

Light	Lumière
Turn the **light** on.	Allume la **lumière.**

Luh-mee-eh-ruh

Money	Argent
Spend your **money** wisely.	Dépense ton **argent** de façon intelligente.

R-gan

Bed	Lit
This **bed** is comfortable.	Ce **lit** est confortable.

Lee

Window	Fenêtre
That **window** points south.	Cette **fenêtre** donne côté sud.

Fuh-neh-truh

Water	Eau
I want some **water**.	Je veux de l'**eau.**

oh

Car	Voiture
That is a nice **car**.	C'est une belle **voiture**.

Voo-ah-tur

Bicycle	Vélo
I took your **bicycle.**	J'ai pris ton **vélo**.

Veh-loh

Photo	Photo
I have your **photo** in my wallet.	J'ai ta **photo** dans mon porte-monnaie.

Foh-toh

News	Actualités
Did you read the **news**?	Tu as lu les **actualités**?

Ak-tu-ah-lee-the

"Les actualités" are very important to keep you informed.

Let me give you a little advice. When preparing to visit another country, you could start reading local news sources from that country a couple of weeks before you get there. That will give you an insight into what is happening in the country and – why not – also some great talking points when you are speaking with locals.

Bin	Poubelle
I put it all in that **bin**.	J'ai tout mis à la **poubelle**.

Poo-bel-uh

Toothbrush	Brosse à dents
I need a new **toothbrush**.	J'ai besoin d'une nouvelle **brosse à dents.**

Bross-ah-dan

Mirror	Miroir
That **mirror** looks dirty.	Ce **miroir** à l'air sale.

Mee-rwar

Laptop	Ordinateur portable
You can use my **laptop**.	Tu peux utliser mon **ordinateur portable.**

Or-dee-nah-tur por-tah-bluh

Computer	Ordinateur
That is my **computer**.	Ça, c'est mon **ordinateur**.

www.LearnLikeNatives.com

Or-dee-nah-tur

Cellphone	Téléphone portable
I don't find my **cellphone**.	Je ne trouve pas mon **portable**.

Por-tah-bluh

Id	Carte d'identité
Please, let me see your **id**.	Faites-moi voir votre **carte d'identité,** s'il-vous plaît.

Car-tuh dee-dan-tee-teh

Driving license	Permis de conduire
You look funny in your **license**.	Tu es marrant sur la photo de ton **permis de conduire**.

Per-mee duh con-duee-ruh

Wallet	Porte-monnaie
Did you find your **wallet**?	As-tu trouvé ton **porte-monnaie**?

Por-tuh-mo-neh

www.LearnLikeNatives.com

Are you ready to create your own list? How many of those things are there in your house? Ok, let us take an example to understand it better.

Nancy: *Honey! Do you have everything you need for camp?*

Chéri! Tu as tout ce dont tu as besoin pour la colonie?

Peter: *Yes, mom. I think so.*

Oui maman, je crois.

Nancy: *Do you have your id and cellphone?*

Tu as ta carte d'identité et ton portable?

Peter: *Yes. I cannot find my toothbrush.*

Oui. Je ne trouve pas ma brosse à dents.

Nancy: *I saw it by the bathroom mirror.*

Je l'ai vue près du miroir de la salle de bains.

Peter: *Thanks! Can I bring my laptop?*

	Merci! Est-ce que je peux amener mon ordinateur portable?
Nancy:	*To camp? No! Bring your wallet. You need that.*
	A la colonie? Non! Prends ton porte-monnaie.
Peter:	*I need money, too.*
	J'ai besoin d'argent, aussi.
Nancy:	*It is on your bed.*
	C'est sur ton lit.
Peter:	*Good. I also need water and a small bin.*
	Parfait. J'ai également besoin d'eau et d'une petite poubelle.
Nancy:	*A bin? Why?*
	Une poubelle? Pourquoi?
Peter:	*For the food. Haven't you read the news? It's bear season.*

	Pour la nourriture. Tu n'as pas lu les actualités? C'est la saison des ours.
Nancy:	*Really? Ok. Keep your light close to you, just in case.*
	Vraiment? Ok. Gardes la lumière près de toi, juste au cas ou.
Peter:	*Sure. Thanks, mom.*
	Bien-sûr. Merci, maman.

It is getting easier; I can feel it. I promise you that if you follow the instructions and keep repeating our little lessons, you will have great results. Feel free to go back to the previous chapters as many times as you like, and you will become fluent in no time!

If you need help to count how many times you are repeating a sentence, move on to the next chapter: we are going to learn numbers next!

www.LearnLikeNatives.com

Chapter 6 – How far can you count?

There are many nursery rhymes that help to introduce numbers even before a child understands numbers or how to count. It was probably through one of these songs that many of us learned numbers and measurements.

That is what we will learn in this chapter. Don't worry. You won't have to do any math!

When speaking in French, you will often need to use and understand numbers to express time, record dates and – of course – count. So here is a table to help you memorize them:

		Pronunciation
One	Un	Uhn
Two	Deux	Duh
Three	Trois	Troowa
Four	Quatre	Katr
Five	Cinq	Cenk

Six	Six	Sees
Seven	Sept	Set
Eight	Huit	Oo-eet
Nine	Neuf	Nuhf
Ten	Dix	Dis
Eleven	Onze	Onz
Twelve	Douze	Dooz
Thirteen	Treize	Trehz
Fourteen	Quatorze	Ka-toh-rz
Fifteen	Quinze	Kenz
Sixteen	Seize	Sez

As you can see, all the numbers from one to sixteen are specific words, and as such you will have to learn it by hear. From seventeen to nineteen, numbers are formed from the root "dix-") meaning ten.

Seventeen	Dix-sept	Dee-set
Eighteen	Dix-huit	Dee-zoo-eet
Nineteen	Dix-neuf	Dee-z-nuhf

All compound numbers are formed adding the ten and the unit. You could read these numbers as "ten eight", i.e. "Dix-huit".

The same goes for numbers from 21 to 29. We just take the root number (vingt) and add the unit.

Twenty	Vingt	Ven
Twenty one	Vingt-et-un	Ven-the-uhn
Twenty two	Vingt-deux	Ven-tuh-duh
Twenty three	Vingt-trois	Ven-troo-ah
Twenty four	Vingt-quatre	Vent-kah-truh
Twenty five	Vingt-cinq	Vent-senk
Twenty six	Vingt-six	Vent-sees

Twenty seven	Vingt-sept	Vent-set
Twenty eight	Vingt-huit	Vent-hueet
Twenty nine	Vingt-neuf	Vent-nuhf

Note how twenty-one is slightly different, as French people say "vingt-et-un", meaning "twenty-and-one". Same goes for thirty-one, forty-one etc… For the other numbers, the "and" is not used.

Thirty	Trente	Tran-tuh
Thirty one	Trente-et-un	Tran-teh-euhn
Thirty two	Trente-deux	Tran-tuh-duh
Fourty	Quarante	Kah-ran-tuh
Fifty	Cinquante	Sen-kan-tuh
Sixty	Soixante	Soo-ah-san-tuh
Seventy	Soixante-dix	Soo-ah-san-tuh dees
Eighty	Quatre-vingt	Kah-truh-ven

Ninety	Quatre-vingt-dix	Kah-truh-ven-this
One hundred	Cent	san
One thousand	Mille	Meel

Any non-native French person learning the language will agree that one of the trickiest things to get to grips with is the number system.

It might be smooth sailing until you get to sixty-nine, but then funny things start to happen because they don't have a separate word for seventy, or eighty, or even ninety for that matter.

Soixante-dix (70) literally means "sixty-ten," *soixante et onze* (71) means "sixty and eleven," *soixante-douze* (72) means "sixty-twelve," etc.

Likewise, there's no word for "eighty" in standard French.* The French say *quatre-vingts*, literally four-twenties.** So 81 is *quatre-vingt-un* (four-twenty-one), 82 is *quatre-vingt-deux* (four-twenty-two), etc.

In keeping with the general weirdness at this end of the number scale, there's no standard French word for ninety* either; it follows the same pattern as 70. That is, you continue using *quatre-vingt* and adding from ten. 90 is *quatre-vingt-dix* (four-twenty-ten), 91 is *quatre-vingt-onze* (four-twenty-eleven), etc.

In some French-speaking areas, such as Belgium and Switzerland, "seventy" is *septante* and "ninety" is *nonante*. As for 80, Belgium uses the standard *quatre-vingts*, while Switzerland uses *huitante*. There's also an archaic word *octante* that you might hear in Switzerland.

Let's move on to ordinal numbers. As the name suggests, they tell the "order" of things. These numbers show rank or position.

First	Premier	Pruh-mee-eh
Second	Second	Suh-guon
Third	Troisième	Troo-ah-zee-m
Fourth	Quatrième	Ka-tree-m
Fifth	Cinquième	Sen-kee-m
Sixth	Sixième	See-z-m

Seventh	Septième	Set-ee-m
Eighth	Huitième	Hueet-m
Nineth	Neuvième	Nuh-vee-m
Tenth	Dixième	Dee-zee-m

As is the case with cardinal numbers, each of the first ten ordinal numbers has a distinct form. Form eleventh onward, ordinal numbers are formed by dropping the final vowel of the number and adding the suffix –ième.

Eleventh	Onzième	Onz-ee-m
Twelfth	Douzième	Dooz-ee-m
Thirteenth	Treizième	Trez-ee-m
Fourteenth	Quatorzième	Ka-tor-zee-m
Fifteenth	Quinzième	Ken-zee-m
Twentieth	Vingtième	Ven-tee-m

Have you seen how easy it is to create ordinal numbers? I know it's not a competition, but why not try to get there first?

Chapter 7 – What did you want to be when you grew up?

What did you want to be when you grew up?" How many times did someone ask you this question when you were a child? And how many times have you changed your answer?

When I was little, I wanted to be a scientist. Later on, I wanted to be a singer. Nowadays, I am a writer, but previously I have had different jobs. I have been a teacher, an electrician – honestly, not a very good one- and a chef.

We always need to remember that all professions are important. We need farmers to produce food of the highest quality, doctors to treat injuries and disease, artists to represent the beauty of the world around us.

Speaking of artists, this is a good word to start with.

Artist	Artiste
Manet was an **artist.**	Manet était un **artiste.**

R-tees-tuh

You should always keep in mind that vowels like "a" are very open and clear in . "A" is pronounced like the English word "ah!". "Artiste"

Chef	Chef/ Chef de cuisine
I want to become a **chef**.	Je veux devenir un **chef de cuisine.**

Sh-eh-f

Construction worker	Ouvrier
My dad is a **construction worker**.	Mon père est un **ouvrier**.

Oo-vree-eh

Firefighter	Pompier
Being a **firefighter** is a risky job.	**Pompier** est un emploi risqué.

Pom-pee-eh

Doctor	Docteur
The **doctor** will see you in 5 minutes.	Le **docteur** vous reçevra dans 5 minutes.

Doc-tuh-r

Policeman	Policier
A **policeman** came to our house.	Un **policier** est venu à la maison.

Po-lee-see-eh

Teacher	Enseignant
That is my **teacher**.	Voici mon **enseignant**.

An-seh-nee-an

Actor/Actress	Acteur/Actrice
Emma Stone is an **actress**.	Emma Stone est une **actrice**.

Ac-trees

Banker	Banquier
I am waiting for a **banker**.	J'attends un **banquier**.

Ban-kee-eh

| Butcher | Boucher |

| I am calling the **butcher** to order. | J'appelle le **boucher** pour commander. |

Boo-sh-eh

| Dentist | Dentiste |
| I have a great **dentist.** | J'ai un **dentiste** formidable. |

Den-tees-tuh

| Driver | Conducteur |
| My **driver** is very fast. | Mon **conducteur** va très vite. |

Kon-duk-tuhr

Are you making any progress?

| Electrician | Electricien |
| You need to call the **electrician**. | Tu dois appeler l'**electricien**. |

Eh-lehk-tree-see-ehn

Farmer	Agriculteur
My grandpa was a **farmer**.	Mon grand-père était un **agriculteur**.

Ah-gree-cul-tuhr

Hairdresser	Coiffeur/Coiffeuse
I have a great **hairdresser**.	J'ai un excellent **coiffeur**.

Kwa-fuhr

Journalist	Journaliste
I will be a **journalist**.	Je serais un **journaliste**.

Joor-nah-lee-stuh

Lawyer	Avocat
My daughter is a **lawyer**.	Ma fille est une **avocate**.

Ahv-voh-ka-tuh

Painter	Peintre
That **painter** did a good job.	Ce **peintre** a fait un bon travail.

Pen-truh

There are plenty of professions but don't worry, we won't go through them all. Just a few more words.

Politician	Politicien
I want to be a **politician**.	Je veux être un **politicien**.

Po-lee-tee-see-en

Psychologist	Psychologue
I am a **psychologist**.	Je suis un **psychologue**.

Psee-ko-lo-guh

Scientist	Scientifique
Scientists are addressing climate change.	Les **scientifiques** s'intéressent au changement climatique.

See-an-tee-feek

What did you want to be when you grew up? Let's learn few more words.

Plumber	Plombier

| I have to call the **plumber**. | Je dois appeler le **plombier**. |

Ploh-meh-roh

| Secretary | Secretaire |
| My **secretary** is on vacation. | Ma **secrétaire** est en vacances. |

Suh-creh-ter

| Shoemaker | Cordonnier |
| The **shoemaker** did a good job. | Le **cordonnier** a fait du bon travail. |

Kor-doh-nee-eh

| Singer | Chanteur |
| She's a great **singer**. | Elle est une bonne **chanteuse**. |

Shan-tuh-zuh

| Waiter/Waitress | Serveur/Serveuse |

| I'll call the **waiter**. | Je vais appeler le **serveur**. |

Ser-vuhr

| Writer | Ecrivain |
| It is hard to be a **writer**. | C'est difficile d'être un **écrivain**. |

Eh-kree-vein

| Translator | Traducteur |
| I work as a **translator**. | Je travaille en tant que **traducteur**. |

Tra-duk-tuhr

Ready for a dialogue?

Cris: *Hey! What do you have there?*

Salut! Qu'est-ce que tu as là?

Layla: *It's a firefighter costume.*

C'est un costume de pompier

Cris: *Is November yet?*

On est déjà en Novembre?

Layla: *No! My son's school is going to have a "career day".*

Non! L'école de mon fils organise une journée des métiers.

Cris: *Oh, I see. I wanted to be a psychologist when I was nine.*

Oh, je vois. Je voulais être un pychologue quand j'avais neuf ans.

Layla: *I wanted to be a teacher. We are always changing, right?*

Je voulais être enseignant. Nous changeons tout le temps d'avis, pas vrai?

Cris: *Yeah. I wanted to be a teacher when I was fourteen.*

Oui. Je voulais être enseignant quand j'avais quatorze ans.

Layla: *How did you decide to become a lawyer?*

Comment as-tu décidé de devenir avocat?

Cris: *Well… you know. I was seventeen and wanted to change the world.*

Ben… Tu sais. J'avais dix-sept ans et je voulais changer le monde.

Layla: *My son wants to be a farmer.*

Mon fils veut être agriculteur.

Cris: *Is his mother not a politician?*

Sa mère n'est elle pas politicienne?

Layla: *Yeah. She started as a journalist and then changed careers.*

Si. Elle a commence en tant que journaliste puis elle a changée de carrière.

Cris: *Indeed. We are always changing.*

C'est vrai. On change tout le temps.

Now, repeat with me: "I wanted to be" -"je voulais être" and complete the sentence.

One of the first questions people ask to someone they have just meet is "What is your job?" which translates to "Quel est ton métier?" Thanks to what we have just learned in this unit, you are going to be ready for this conversation!

What next? Let's go to learn how to give directions.

Chapter 8 – Where are we going?

Be able to clearly tell where you want to go is very important, especially when traveling in another country. For this reason, have the ability to communicate in simple situations such as asking for directions can make your life easier, in case of a SatNav failure or during a relaxing afternoon walk when you don't have your mobile with you.

Street	La rue
That is the main **street**.	C'est la rue principale.

ruh

Avenue	Avenue
This is Clemenceau **Avenue**.	Voici l'**Avenue** Clémenceau.

A-vuh-nu

Block	Quartier

We are going to the **block** party.	Nous allons à la fête du **quartier**.

Kar-tee-eh

Square	Place
The **square** shouldn't be far from here.	La **place** ne devrait pas être très loin.

Plah-ssuh

Building	Immeuble
This **building** has 110 floors.	Cet **immeuble** a 110 étages.

E-mub-luh

Monument	Monument
This **monument** is 300 years old.	Ce **monument** a 300 ans.

Moh-nuh-man

Hospital	Hopital
The **hospital** is 5 minutes away.	L'**hopital** est à 5 minutes d'ici.

Ho-p-tal

Corner	Angle
The store is passing that **corner.**	Le magasin est après cet **angle**.

An-gluh

Nearest	Le plus proche
That is the **nearest** mall.	Voici le centre commercial le **plus proche**.

Pluh-proh-shuh

Turn left	Tourner à gauche
You should **turn left** here.	Tu devrais **tourner à gauche** ici.

Toor-neh-ah-goh-shuh

Turn right	Tourner à droite
Let's **turn right** after this corner.	**Tournons à droite** à cet angle.

Toor-neh-ah-droo-what

Go straight on	Aller tout droit

You only have to **go straight** on and you will get there.	Tu dois seulement **aller tout droit** et tu y arriveras.

Ah-leh-too-droo-ah

Go past	Dépasser
You have to **go past** the main street.	Tu dois **dépasser** l'avenue principale.

Deh-pah-seh

Crossroads	Intersection
Take the left on the **crossroads**.	Prenez à gauche à l'**intersection**.

N-tehr-sec-see-on

Those phrases will take you wherever you desire! Are you ready to put into practice what we have just learned about directions?

John: *Hey, sir! Good afternoon.*

Bonjour, monsieur !

Vendor: **(Vendeur)**	*What can I do for you?* *Que puis-je faire pour vous?*
John:	*Can you tell me how I can get to the train station?* *Est-ce que vous pouvez me dire comment me rendre à la gare?*
Vendor	*Sure. You have to go in that direction for 300m.* *Bien-sûr. Vous devez prendre cette direction pendant 300m.*
John:	*I have to go past the library?* *Est-ce que je dois dépasser la bibliothèque?*
Vendor	*Yes. Then, you turn left and go for another five or six hundred meters.* *Oui. Après, vous tournez à gauche et avancer encore cinq ou six-cent mètres.*
John:	*Oh, I think I come from there. But I got confused at the crossroads.*

	Oh. Je crois que je viens de là-bas. Mais j'étais confus à l'intersection.
Vendor	*Very usual. You have to take a left at the crossroads.*
	C'est normal. Vous devez prendre à gauche à l'intersection.
John:	*Ok.*
	D'accord.
Vendor	*You will see a square. The station is in front.*
	Vous verrez une place. La gare est en face.
John:	*Thank you very much.*
	Merci beaucoup.
Vendor:	*Don't worry. Have a nice trip.*
	Pas de problème. Bon voyage.

Are you ready to go and explore a new place? Better hurry! "Survival 101" is coming.

www.LearnLikeNatives.com

Chapter 9 – Survival 101

Each chapter contains helpful information, but this is particularly important. We have already said that: things do happen. Your child may feel unwell, you could twist an ankle while hiking, lose your passport... things do happen. So it's better to be prepared, right?

I believe that this sentence in particular is fundamental for you:

| Do you speak English? | Parlez-vous Anglais? |

Par-leh-voo-an-gleh

That is a question you should always remember, as could make your life much easier.

| Where is the bathroom? | Où sont les toilettes? |

oo-son-leh-twah-let

| How can I get to this place? | Comment puis-je me rendre à cet endroit? |

www.LearnLikeNatives.com

Ko-man-puee-juh-muh-ran-druh-ah-set-an-droo-ah

| Where is the nearest hospital? | Où se trouve l'hôpital le plus proche? |

Oo-suh-troo-vuh-loh-pee-tal-luh-plu-proh-shuh

| When is the next flight? | Quand est le prochain vol? |

Kaan-eh-luh-proh-chen-vol

| Who can I talk to about this problem? | A qui puis-je parler de ce problème? |

Ah-kee-puh-ee-juh-par-leh-duh-suh-proh-blem

| Where can I find a policeman? | Où est-ce que je peux trouver un policier? |

Oo-eh-suh-kuh-juh-puh-troo-veh-un-poh-lee-cee-eh

Though I hope you will never need this:

| Where is the embassy? | Où se trouve l'embassade? |

oo-suh-troo-vuh-lam-bah-sah-duh

| What do I need to visit...? | Qu'est-ce que je devrais visiter...? |

Keh-suh-kuh-juh-duh-vreh-v-z-teh

| Where can I find...? | Où puis-je trouver ...? |

Oo-puee-juh-troo-veh

Oh, I really hope you won't need any of them. But better safe than sorry! Let's see a short dialogue now.

Harry: *Hello, sir. How can I get to Kapital Burger, in Clemenceau Avenue?*

Bonjour Monsieur. Comment puis-je me rendre au Kapital Burger, à l'avenue Clémenceau?

Driver: *I can take you, but it is far. Is someone waiting for you? It's rush hour.*

Je peux vous y amener, mais c'est loin. Quelqu'un vous attends? C'est l'heure de pointe.

Harry: *No. I think I left my passport there.*

Non. Je crois que j'ai laissé mon passeport là-bas.

Driver: *It will take us at least 40 minutes to get there.*

Ça nous prendra au moins 40 minutes pour y aller.

Harry: Ok. Maybe I can talk to someone there.

D'accord. Peut-être que je peux parler à quelqu'un là-bas.

Vendor: Good afternoon. Kapital Burger.

Bonjour. Kapital Burger.

Harry: Hello! My name is Harry Klein. I was there last night, and I think I left my passport.

Bonjour! Je m'appelle Harry Klein. J'ai dîné chez vous hier soir et je crois que j'ai laissé mon passeport.

Vendor: One second, please. Do you remember where you were sitting?

Une seconde, s'il vous plaît. Vous vous rappelez de l'endroit où vous étiez assis?

Harry: Yes. I was at the bar, by the corner.

Oui. J'étais au bar, dans l'angle.

Vendor: Ok. Give me a second.

	D'accord. Donnez moi une seconde.
Harry:	Ok.
	Ok.
Vendor:	*Yeah. I just consulted my coworkers and they did not find anything. I am sorry.*
	Oui. Je viens de demander à mes collègues et ils n'ont rien trouvé. Je suis désolé.
Harry:	*Thank you.*
	Merci
Driver:	*They didn't find it?*
	Ils ne l'ont pas trouvé?
Harry:	*No. Where is the nearest police station?*
	Non. Où est le commissariat le plus proche?
Driver:	*Don't you want to go to your embassy? Could be better.*
	Vous ne voulez pas aller à votre embassade? Ce serait mieux.
Harry:	*Oh, yes. Where's the UK embassy?*

Oh, oui. Où est l'embassade du Royaume-Uni?

Driver: *Actually, it is near from here. We will be there in a few minutes.*

C'est près d'ici. Nous y serons dans quelques minutes.

What a nightmare to lose your passport abroad! I sincerely hope you never have to use any of these phrases.

Now, let's move on to something less stressful. Shall we switch to colors?

Chapter 10 – What is the color of the sky?

I will tell you a secret: I love a wonderful view, and everywhere I go, I like just to lose myself gazing at the sky. I particularly love the sunset. I also like the sunrise, but I'm not really a morning person.

How many colors are there in the sky?

Yellow	Jaune
My dress is **yellow**.	Ma robe est **jaune**.

Joh-nuh

Blue	Bleu
The sky looks very **blue**.	Le ciel à l'air très **bleu**.

Bluh

Red	Rouge
I bought a **red** car.	J'ai acheté une voiture **rouge**.

Roo-guh

Purple	Violet
Those flowers are **purple.**	Ces fleurs sont **violettes**.

V-oh-let-uh

Pink	Rose
My daughter wants a **pink** skirt.	Ma fille veut une jupe **rose**.

Roh-suh

Green	Vert
The fields look very **green** this year.	Les champs ont l'air très **verts** cette année.

Ver

Orange	Organge
I want my **orange** t-shirt.	Je veux mon t-shirt **orange**.

Oh-ran-guh

Brown	Marron
Your dog is **brown**.	Ton chien est **marron**.

Mah-ron

Grey	Gris
Grey is a mixed color.	Le **gris** est une couleur mixte.

Gree

Black	Noir
Black is my favorite color.	Le **noir** est ma couleur préférée.

Noo-r

White	Blanc
I painted the walls **white**.	J'ai peint les murs en **blanc**.

Blan

Fun fact: black and white are not colors. They represent, respectively, the absence of light and the lack of shadow.

Let's look at an example.

Lisa: *Hey, honey! I need your help with something.*

Hey, chéri! J'ai besoin de ton aide avec quelque chose.

Alex: Yes, love. What is it?

Oui, mon amour. Qu'est-ce qu'il y a?

Lisa: We need to pick the colors for the house before we move.

Nous devons choisir les couleurs pour la maison avant le déménagement.

Alex: Oh, true. What do you have in mind?

Oh, c'est vrai. Qu'est-ce que tu as en tête?

Lisa: I was thinking of a light blue for our room, with touches of yellow.

Je pensais à du bleu clair pour notre chambre, avec des touches de jaune.

Alex: Ok. What have you thought of the living room?

D'accord. A quoi tu penses pour le salon?

Lisa: I am thinking of a combination of red and white walls.

Je pense à une combinaison de murs rouges et blancs.

Alex: *Do you think that my black chair will match?*

Tu penses que ma chaise noire ira bien avec ça?

Lisa: *Positive. And for the studio, I was looking for something more neutral.*

Certainement. Et pour le studio, je cherchais quelque chose de plus neutre.

Alex: *By neutral you mean…?*

Par neutre tu veux dire…?

Lisa: *Earth colors. Like a light brown.*

Des couleurs de la terre. Comme un marron clair.

Alex: *And the nursery?*

Et la chambre du bébé?

Lisa: *Grey, with a purple wall.*

Gris, avec un mur violet.

Alex: *It sounds amazing. Thanks for planning all this.*

Ça à l'air génial. Merci d'avoir pensé à tout ça.

Lisa: *Sure! I love it!*

Avec Plaisir! J'adore!

What about you? Are you already planning to repaint your whole house? And for your dining room, would you like to go and buy some lanterns at an artisanal market in Paris? Imagine all the things you could do! First of all, however, we need to get there. Shall we just do that?

Chapter 11 – So much to do, so much to see

Where do you dream of going? Personally, I love the mountains. I grew up in a village in the valley, with a stunning view of the mountains. I think maybe that's why I love mountains so much! But anyway, enough about me.

Now, imagine where you would like to go…

Travel	Voyager
She lost the scarf during her last **travel**.	Elle a perdu son echarpe lors de son dernier **voyage**.

Voo-ah-ya-guh

Ticket	Billet
I bought a two-way **ticket**.	J'ai acheté un **billet** aller retour.

B-eh

Airplane	Avion

| This **airplane** is big. | Cet **avion** est grand. |

Ah-v-on

| Reservation | Réservation |
| He made a **reservation** for tonight. | Il a fait une **réservation** pour cette nuit. |

Reh-zer-vah-see-on

| Hotel | Hotel |
| I like this **hotel**. | J'aime bien cet **hotel**. |

Ho-tel

| Room | Chambre |
| They need a double **room**. | Ils ont besoin d'une **chambre** double. |

Sham-bruh

| Key | Clef |
| I lost my **key**. | J'ai perdu ma **clef**. |

Kleh

| Passport | Passeport |

| Can I see your **passport**? | Puis-je voir votre **passeport**? |

Pah-spor

| Taxi | Taxi |
| Let's take a **taxi**. | Prenons un **taxi**. |

Tac-si

"Taxi" is the same both in French and in English.

| Car rental | Location de voiture |
| Where is the **car rental**? | Où se trouve le bureau de **location de voiture?** |

Loh-kah-see-on

| Bus | Bus |
| We will take the **bus**. | Nous allons prendre le **bus**. |

Bus

| Subway | Metro |
| The subway was out of service. | Le **metro** était hors service. |

Meh-troh

Train	Train
I'll take the **train**.	Je prendrai le **train**.

Tren

Station	Station
That is the nearest **station**.	Voici la **station** la plus proche.

Stah-see-on

Theater	Théâtre
This **theater** was remodeled 5 years ago.	Ce **théâtre** a été reconstruit il y a 5 ans.

Teh-ah-truh

Beach	Plage
She wants to go to the **beach**.	Elle veut aller à la **plage**.

Pla-guh

Mountain	Montagne

www.LearnLikeNatives.com

| They want to climb that **mountain.** | Ils veulent grimper cette **montagne.** |

Mon-ta-nee-uh

| Island | Ile |
| Let's go to that **island**. | Allons sur cette **île**. |

Eel

| City | Ville |
| Canada has big **cities**. | Le Canada a des grandes **villes**. |

Veel-luh

Are you ready? You know what's coming next!

Shaun: *I want to buy the tickets for our travel. Can we decide on something?*

Je veux acheter les billets pour notre voyage. On peut se mettre d'accord?

Vanessa: *Sure! Where do we want to go?*

	Bien-sûr. Où est-ce qu'on veut aller?
Shaun:	*Not another city. I want to rest.*
	Pas encore une ville. Je veux me reposer.
Vanessa:	*I agree. Do you remember that beautiful mountain that Lisa showed us? Navarino Island.*
	Je suis d'accord. Tu te rappelles de cette montagne magnifique que Lisa nous a montrée? L'île de Navarino.
Shaun:	*Oh, sure. That cozy mountain house, right?*
	Ah, bien-sûr. La maison de montagne chaleureuse, c'est ça?
Vanessa:	*Yes. That one.*
	Oui. C'est ça.
Shaun:	*That sounds great. Do you think it is available?*
	Ça à l'air génial. Tu penses que c'est disponible?
Vanessa:	*On it!*

	Je suis dessus!
Shaun:	*Remember to check for a view.*
	Rappelles-toi de regarder s'il y a une vue.
Vanessa:	*I got the perfect room! It is beautiful.*
	J'ai trouvé la chambre parfaite! Elle est magnifique.
Shaun:	*Great. I need our passports to buy the tickets. I'll go get them.*
	Super. J'ai besoin de nos passeports pour acheter les billets. Je vais les chercher.
Vanessa:	*Sure. I am excited!*
	D'accord. Je suis super excitée!

So, are you getting excited?

Repeat with me: "je veux voyager –I want to travel-, and make it happen. Traveling is an amazing way to meet new people and discover beautiful places. In my opinion, traveling is growing up and you can never end it!

A spontaneous trip, a last-second vacation… these are usually the best things. These are the kind of stories you will remember forever. Some memories are just amazing!

And do you know what else I like when traveling? The food!

www.LearnLikeNatives.com

A Quick Message

A quick message before we start the final chapter of this book.

"No one can whistle a symphony. It takes a whole orchestra to play it." –

H.E. Luccock

Do you want to be part of the orchestra of the Learning Spanish community?

Here is how:

If you're enjoying this book, I would like to kindly ask you to leave a brief review on Amazon.

Reviews aren't easy to come by, but they have a profound impact in supporting my work. This way, I can keep creating new content to help the whole community at my very best.

I would be incredibly thankful if you could just take a minute to leave a quick review on Amazon, even if it's just a sentence or two!

It's that simple!

www.LearnLikeNatives.com

Thank you so much for taking the time to leave a short review on Amazon.

The community and I are very appreciative, as your review makes a difference.

Now, let's get back to learning Spanish!

Chapter 12 : I am a bit hungry

French people are known for their gastronomy and set amazingly high culinary standards. The French have been the leaders and are recognized as innovators in the culinary arts scene since the beginning of time.

Most of the famous chefs in history are French. We could cite a few such as Paul Bocuse, Joël Robuchon, or Anne-Sophie Pic. The well known and famous chefs that are not French, nevertheless, are mostly trained in the art of cooking « à la Française », the « French-style ». Cooking knowledge and skills required to prepare a good meal is something that the French people take excessive pride in when they present meals.

France has many culinary regions, and each one has a specific characteristic of its own food and area. Generally, French food requires the use of many different types of sauces and gravies. The northwestern region of France produces recipes for cuisine that tend to require ingredients like apples, milk, butter, and cream, and the meals tend to be extremely rich and sometimes rather heavy. Reminiscent of the German style of food, the southeastern area of France, the French cuisine is heavy in lard and meat products such as sauerkraut and pork sausage.

The more widely accepted type of French food is southern French Mediterranean cuisine. This type of food is often served in traditional French restaurants. The dishes are a lot lighter in fat in the southeastern area of France. In the southeast area of France, culinary creations tend to lean more toward the side of a light olive oil than any other type of oil and usually don't use butter. Also, they rely heavily on herbs and tomatoes, as well as tomato-based products.

Cooking is an essential part of French culture, like sharing a meal and a good bottle of wine. French people find quality time, good food, and drinks, really important.

Are you ready to practice?

Tomato	Tomate
You only need a few **tomatoes**.	Tu as seulement besoin de quelques **tomates.**

Toh-mah-tuh

This one is not that hard, right? You should know that tomatoes are used in a lot of Mediterranean dishes, so you might want to remember this one.

Corn	Maïs
I love **corn**.	J'adore le **maïs**.

Ma-ees

Egg	Oeuf
She wants **eggs** and ham.	Elle veut des **oeufs** et du jambon.

Jam-bohn

Cheese	Fromage
I don't eat **cheese**.	Je ne mange pas de **fromage**.

Froh-mah-guh

Cheese is also VERY important in the French culture.

Butter	Beurre
French people love **butter.**	Les français aiment le **beurre**.

Buh-rruh

Sandwich	Sandwich
We want five regular **sandwiches**.	Nous aimerions avoir cinq **sandwich** classiques.

Sand-weesh

Burger	Hamburger
They want three **burgers**.	Ils veulent trois **hamburgers**.

Ham-bur-gher

Salad	Salade
I want a Caesar **salad.**	Je veux une **salade** César.

Sa-lah-duh

Shrimp	Crevettes

| It has **shrimps** inside. | Il y a des **crevettes** à l'intérieur. |

Kruh-vet-uh

Sausage	Saucisse
We love **sausages** for breakfast.	Nous adorons la **saucisse** au petit-déjeuner.

So-see-suh

Bread	Pain
I bought the **bread** this morning.	J'ai acheté le **pain** ce matin.

Pein

As you know, you will find bakeries in almost every French village, where you can order the most famous French bread, "la baguette".

Of course, you will also find pastries, "pâtisseries" and "viennoiseries", such as "croissants" and "pain au chocolat", to enjoy your breakfast.

www.LearnLikeNatives.com

As for bread, it is a tradition in France to always have some in the middle of the table, for people to share during their meal. Most of the time, it is a "baguette", or a similar type of bread.

Chicken	Poulet
That **chicken** is raw.	Ce **poulet** est crû.

Poo-leh

Pancakes	Pancakes
These **pancakes** are fluffy.	Ces **pancakes** sont moelleux.

Pan-keh-kes

Rice	Riz
The **rice** is ready.	Le **riz** est prêt

Ree

Beef	Boeuf
The flavor of the **beef** is delicious.	La saveur du **boeuf** est délicieuse.

Beh-kon

The French, like Italian and Spanish people, eat a lot of red meat and have the best recipes to make it melt in your mouth. Hungry yet?

Milk	Lait
I think this **milk** has gone bad.	Je crois que ce **lait** n'est plus bon.

Leh

Cake	Gâteau
You can eat more **cake**.	Tu peux manger plus de **gâteau**.

Gah-toh

Soup	Soupe
This **soup** is hot.	Cette **soupe** est chaude.

Soo-puh

"Onion soup" is a famous dish in France, mostly served as a starter.

Onion	Onion
I was chopping **onions**.	Je découpais des **onions**.

Oh-nee-on

Garlic	Ail
You need to add **garlic** and stir.	Tu dois rajouter de l'**ail** et touiller.

Ah-ee

Garlic, onions and olive oil, are often used in French dishes, especially southern ones!

Lemon	Citron
These **lemons** look very nice.	Ces **citrons** ont l'air très bons.

C-trohn

Orange	Orange

| I want **orange** juice, please. | J'aimerais du jus d'orange, s'il-vous plaît. |

Oh-ran-guh

Peanut	Cacahuète
I am allergic to **peanuts**.	Je suis allergique aux **cacahuètes**.

Kah-Kah-oo-ett

"Cacahuète" is an important one. It is, after all, one of the most common food allergies.

We are almost done with this first level!

Just one more conversation! Let's go!

Veronica: *I am hungry.*

J'ai faim.

Karol: *Let's see. There are still eggs, cheese and bread from breakfast.*

	Voyons voir. Il y a encore des oeufs, du fromage et du pain du petit-déjeuner.
Veronica:	*Uhm... Do we have potatoes and onions? They can be good with eggs.*
	Uhm... Est-ce que nous avons des patates et des onions? Ce serait bien avec les oeufs.
Karol:	*No. I could not go grocery shopping yesterday.*
	Non. Je n'ai pas pu aller faire les courses hier.
Veronica:	*It is fine. Maybe I could go to the bakery by the corner.*
	C'est pas grave. Peut-être que je pourrais aller à la boulangerie, à l'angle.
Karol:	*I don't think it is open today.*
	Je ne crois pas que ce soit ouvert aujour'dhui.
Veronica:	*Oh... I could go for a piece of beef, then. The brasserie next door offers take away meals. They're delicious. Do you want anything?*

> Oh… j'aurais bien envie d'une côte de boeuf, alors. La brasserie d'à côté propose des plats à emporter. Ils sont délicieux. Tu veux quelque-chose?

Karol: *That sounds nice! Can you get me a niçoise salad?*

> Bonne idée! Tu peux me prendre une salade niçoise ?

Veronica: *Sure! Anything else?*

> Bien-sûr! Tu veux autre chose?

Karol: *Maybe some sparkling water. They should have Perrier.*

> Peut-être un peu d'eau pétillante. Ils devraient avoir du Perrier.

Veronica: Sounds fine. I will be back soon.

> D'accord. Je reviens bientôt.

I hope it wasn't too difficult as food is very important. Do you agree?

Conclusion

Congratulations, you've made it! See, it wasn't too hard, was it?

As you realized by now, this wasn't your typical language book. If you tried and failed to learn French in the past, you now discovered a new approach, one that you can build on to take your French adventure to the next level. In going away from formal vocabulary and grammar lessons, together we shifted your focus from 'learning' French, to 'speaking' French. Two very different things!

More than just the "rules" of French grammar, today you have a sense of "the soul and music" of the French language. You built a true solid foundation in French and, even if you don't realize it yet, you are now capable of navigating social situations, create connections, keep contacts, as well as make friends. As I mentioned at the start, what's the point in knowing grammatical rules if you can't order your own food!

I won't bore you with the reasons why being able to speak another language is a huge benefit for you. Or why French in particular will open a world of opportunities. I'm sure you're already convinced! But learning a new language is indeed a complex and rich experience, making this book a journey – your journey – into a new culture.

A beautiful culture you're now a part of.

No one is ever 'ready', so get out there! Travel, read fiction and newspapers in French, watch films, eat French foods, make French friends, and immerse yourself in French-speaking cultures. Sure, you'll make a few mistakes at first. But who cares! You can always go back through our lessons and keep building your confidence. I'm sure you'll get there in no time.

This is just the first volume of this series, all packed full of vocabulary and dialogs, covering essential, everyday French that will ensure you master the basics.

You can find the rest of the books in the series, as well as a whole host of other resources, at LearnLikeNatives.com. Simply add the book to your library to take the next step in your language learning journey. If you are ever in need of new ideas or direction, refer to our 'Speak Like a Native' eBook, available to you for free at LearnLikeNatives.com, which clearly outlines practical steps you can take to continue learning any language you choose.

A language should be lived, not just learned. So learn it, live it and, most importantly, enjoy it!

www.LearnLikeNatives.com

www.LearnLikeNatives.com

Learn Like a Native is a revolutionary **language education brand** that is taking the linguistic world by storm. Forget boring grammar books that never get you anywhere, Learn Like a Native teaches you languages in a fast and fun way that actually works!

As an international, multichannel, language learning platform, we provide **books, audio guides and eBooks** so that you can acquire the knowledge you need, swiftly and easily.

Our **subject-based learning**, structured around real-world scenarios, builds your conversational muscle and ensures you learn the content most relevant to your requirements.
Discover our tools at *LearnLikeNatives.com*

When it comes to learning languages, we've got you covered!

www.LearnLikeNatives.com

www.LearnLikeNatives.com

FREE BOOK!

Get the *FREE BOOK* that reveals the secrets path to learn any language fast, and without leaving your country.

Discover:

- The **language 5 golden rules** to master languages at will

- Proven **mind training techniques** to revolutionize your learning

- A complete step-by-step guide to **conquering any language**

www.LearnLikeNatives.com

www.LearnLikeNatives.com

www.LearnLikeNatives.com

Learn French Like a Native *for Beginners - Level 2*

Learning French in Your Car Has Never Been Easier! Have Fun with Crazy Vocabulary, Daily Used Phrases, Exercises & Correct Pronunciations

www.LearnLikeNatives.com

Chapter 1 – Dreaming of the South

You are sitting at home, thinking about vacation, and suddenly a friend calls you to tell you about their latest family travel to the famous "Côte d'Azur" – it was a beautiful, sunny, diverse and entertaining place. You hang up and start imagining yourself with a glass of Chardonnay in hand, the sea in front of you.

Can you imagine shopping with your family through the little streets of world-renowned Cannes? Can you feel the hand of your loved one, the touch, while enjoying a glass of wine at sunset? Just stay with me, because you can have it all.

To make this a reality, the first thing you need to search for are requirements, hotels, and transportation.

English	French
To travel	Voyager

I want **to travel** to Montreal.	Je veux voyager à Montréal.

Vwa-ya-jé

Notice the "oy" sound. For the French language, "oy" or "oi" is almost always pronounced as "wa".

Now repeat: Vwa-ya-jé.

Requirements	Exigences
Requirements to travel to France.	**Les exigences** pour voyager en France.

Eh-guh-zee-gen-suh

Travel stuff	Affaires de voyage
I will need to go buy some travel stuff.	J'aurais besoin d'aller acheter des **affaires de voyage.**

Ah-fer-duh-vwa-ya-guh

This is a typical "difficult" word for English speakers because French has a different "r" sound.

Many French students have trouble with the letter *r*. Follow step-by-step instructions to learn how to pronounce the French *r*:

1. Open your mouth.

2. Close your throat as if you're going to gargle or to avoid swallowing a mouthful of liquid, and say "k" carefully, several times.

3. Pay attention to where in your throat the *k* sound is made. We'll call this the K place.

4. Begin slowly closing your throat until you can almost feel the K place. Your throat should be only partially constricted.

5. Tense the muscles around the K place.

6. Gently push air through your partially-constricted throat.

7. Practice saying "ra-ra-ra" (where r = steps 4-6) every day.

Back to requirements--checking this is very important: due to political and health challenges in many countries, it is possible that you may need some extra requirements to visit, such as vaccines or a travel visa.

Visa	Visa
Do I need a **visa** to travel to France?	Est-ce que j'ai besoin d'un visa pour voyager en France?

Please notice how the word "visa" is the same in both languages, as well as its pronunciation.

Next phrase.

Vaccines	Vaccins
Vaccines are needed to visit French Islands.	Certains **vaccins** sont nécessaires afin de visiter les îles Françaises.

Vak-ssen

"Vaccines" translates as "vaccins", which is almost similar in the written form. However, the pronunciation is not quite the same. This word can be split into two syllables: "vak-ssen".

In case you have these requirements covered, the next step would be to look for flights.

Most airline platforms are multilingual. However, it is known that some domestic flights could be cheaper when bought with a national airline.

Airlines	Compagnies aériennes
What **airlines** travel to Nice?	Quelles **compagnies aériennes** vont à Nice?

Com-pa-nee a-é-ree-ehn-uh

Something to keep in mind is that vowels in French are very open and clear. For example, a French "e" always has a similar sound as the one you would use to say "essay". That starting "e" sound is what we are looking for.

Flights	Vols
Find **flights** from New-York to Paris.	Trouver des **vols** de New-York à Paris.

"vol". The "s" is not pronounced here.

You can notice how the word "from" translates to "de", which is your starting point. While your destination is covered by "à".

One-way trip	Un aller simple
Do you want a **one-way trip**?	Voulez-vous un **aller simple**?

Al-eh sem-pluh

Round trip	Un aller-retour
No, I want a **round trip**.	Non. Je voudrais un **aller-retour.**

Al-eh ruh-toor

Dates	Dates
Dates for your travel?	Les **Dates** de votre voyage?

Repeat after me: Da-tuh. Once again, the "s" is not pronounced.

When looking for accommodations, you have many great references at your disposal, but it is always preferable to ask the locals for specifics related to the best and most touristy locations.

To stay	Loger
Best places **to stay** in Paris.	Les meilleurs endroits où **loger** à Paris.

Lo-jeh

Touristic	Touristique(s)
Most **touristic** places in France.	Les endroits les plus **touristiques** en France.

Too-ree-stee-kuh

Once you have found somewhere you like, the next step is to book a room.

To Book	Réserver
I want to **book** a room.	Je veux **réserver** une chambre.

As you can see, this is another word where you need to put your "r" into training. Repeat after me: reh-zer-veh.

www.LearnLikeNatives.com

Good! Are we acing those r's or what?

Depending on how many people you include in your trip, you could choose a single room or a double room.

Single room	Chambre simple
I want a **single room**.	Je veux une **chambre simple**.

Sham-bruh sem-pluh

Double room	Chambre double.
I want a **double room**.	Je veux une **chambre double**.

Sham-bruh doo-bluh

If you do not enjoy flying, perhaps other transportation methods could be useful.

Cruise	Croisière
I want to go on a **cruise** in the Mediterranean.	Je veux aller en **croisière** dans la Méditerranée.

Crwa-zieh-ruh

How do you feel, so far? Ready to book a trip?

Great! Because now we are going to do some packing.

First, the verb that makes it happen: to pack.

To pack	Faire une valise
I need to **pack** my baggage.	Je dois **faire ma valise**.

Fehr ma va-lee-zuh

There is no actual word for "packing" in French, when it comes to packing a suitcase: Here, the literal translation would be "do a suitcase, or do my suitcase".

With this in mind, repeat again: Je dois faire ma valise.

Of course, you need a suitcase.

Suitcase	Valise
I need a bigger **suitcase**.	J'ai besoin d'une **valise** plus grande.

Va-lee-zuh

The word "valise" can be used in general. However, similar to English, French distinguishes a difference between your checked bags and your carry-on.

Checked bag	Bagage en soute
Your ticket includes one **checked bag**.	Votre ticket inclut un **Bagage en soute**.

Bah-gaj an soo-tuh

Carry-on	Bagage à main
Your **carry-on** is too big.	Votre **bagage à main** est trop grand.

Ba-gaj a mein

Now there is an open suitcase on your bed. It's time to pack!

Shirt	Chemise
I like this **shirt** for the trip.	Cette **chemise** est bien pour le voyage.

Shuh-mee-zuh

T-shirt	T-shirt
Why don't you bring a **t-shirt**? Something more sporty.	Pourquoi ne prendrais-tu pas un **t-shirt**? Quelque chose de plus sportif.

Pants	Pantalon
Should I bring some long **pants**?	Devrais-je enmener un **pantalon** long?

Pan-tah-lon

Shorts	Panta-courts
Maybe I should pack some **shorts**.	Je devrais peut-être enmener des **panta-courts**.

Pan-tah koor

Due to globalization, "shorts" is a common way to call short pants, even in French-speaking countries. Just in case, you have the neutral French way.

Skirt/Dress	Jupe/Robe
I think I will pack a **skirt** and maybe a **dress**.	Je crois que je vais enmener une **jupe** et peut-être une **robe**.

Skirt: ju-puh

Dress: ro-buh

Sweater	Pull
I will bring a **sweater**.	Je vais enmener un **pull**.

Underwear	Sous-vêtements
Pack **underwear** for a week.	Prends des **sous-vêtements** pour une semaine.

Soo-veh-tuh-men

Socks	Chaussettes

| How many **socks** should I bring? | Combien de **chaussettes** devrais-je prendre? |

Shoh-set

And, because we are already on it, it is a good idea to go through some body parts.

| Feet | Pieds |
| You have very cold **feet**. | Tu as des **pieds** très froids. |

Pee-eh

| Legs | Jambes |
| I have to shave my **legs**. | Je dois me raser les **jambes**. |

Jam-buh

| Hands | Mains |
| Do not forget the **hand** cream. | N'oublies pas la crème pour les **mains**. |

mein

Arms	Bras
I want to tan my **arms**.	Je veux bronzer des **bras**.

brah

Head	Tête
I got a bump on my **head**.	J'ai une bosse sur la **tête**.

Teh-tuh

Face	Visage
I need a **face** towel.	J'ai besoin d'une serviette pour mon **visage**.

Vee-zag

How are you doing so far? Are there any words you need to repeat?

Before moving on to a little conversation to practice our first lesson, we should briefly speak about the use of the formal form "Vous". While in English there is no difference between formal and informal, French has a separate form to address others in formal situations. For example, at the doctor, restaurant, when talking to the elderly or addressing strangers. In these cases and any other time you need to show respect or want to be polite, you will use "Vous".

As you will see, it is really easy to create the formal version: all you need to do is conjugate the verb at the second person plural (Vous), instead than using the second person singular (Tu).

To start with, we are looking at a conversation between you and a travel agent. In this example, we will use "Vous" in its formal version.

Agent: *Good afternoon! Where do you want to travel?*

Bonjour! Où souhaitez-vous partir?

Allen: *Nice, France.*

Nice, France.

Agent: *Date for your travel?*

La date de départ?

Allen: *December, 15th.*

Le quinze Décembre.

Agent: *How many adults are traveling?*

Pour combien d'adultes?

Allen: *Two, please.*

Deux, s'il-vous-plaît.

Agent: *Are you traveling with kids?*

Est-ce que vous voyagez avec des enfants?

Allen: *Yes. Two kids.*

Oui. Deux enfants.

Agent: *Would you like a one-way trip or a round trip?*

Souhaitez-vous un aller simple ou un aller-retour?

Allen: *Round trip. Thank you.*

Un aller-retour. Merci.

Agent: *When do you wish to come back?*

Quel jour souhaitez-vous revenir?

Allen: January, 2nd.

Le deux Janvier.

Agent: Okay. Our lowest fare is $350 per person, but it does not include checked bags. Would you like to add checked bags?

D'accord. Notre tarif le plus bas est de $350 par personne, mais ça n'inclut pas de bagages en soute. Voulez-vous en rajouter ?

Allen: Not at the moment. Thank you.

Pas pour le moment, merci.

Agent: Very well. Would you like to book accommodations?

Très bien. Voulez-vous réserver des chambres?

Allen: Sure. What do you have?

Bien-sûr! Qu'est-ce-que vous avez?

Agent: I can offer you two bedrooms. One double with a King size bed, and another double with two single beds.

Je peux vous proposer deux chambres. Une double avec un grand lit double, et une autre avec deux lits simples.

Allen: *Great!*

Super!

Agent: *Perfect. Please, wait in line for a second so I can write down your details.*
Parfait. Veuillez-patienter une seconde pour que je puisse noter vos coordonnées.

How was this for you? Are you feeling more confident now? I hope you do, because we are going to the airport: we have got a plane to catch!

Chapter 2 – Not Only Birds Can Fly

In my experience, airports can be stressful places for multiple reasons. They are crowded spaces with many lines to wait in and documents to show, and you have to do it every single time. Thankfully, I am here to help you be at your gate in time, stress-free.

Let's start by checking you into your flight.

Passport	Passeport
Can I please have your **passport?**	Puis-je voir votre passeport?

Pass-por

The check in desk, offers the ideal opportunity to practice what we learned in chapter one. They are going to ask you where you are traveling to, how many people are traveling with you and the number of bags you wish to check in. Unfortunately, overweight luggage is also a VERY frequent problem.

Overweight	Excédent de bagage.
This piece of luggage is **overweight**.	Ce baggage excède le **poids limité**.

Pwah lee-mee-teh

If you managed to avoid the overweight charges–which I hope, as those fees are usually very high–you are ready to go through security controls.

Tray	Panier
Please take off shoes, coats, and metal objects, and put your belongings in a **tray**.	S'il-vous-plaît, retirez vos chaussures, vos manteaux et tout objets en métal, et mettez vos affaires dans un **panier**.

Pa-nee-eh

Screen	Révision

Please, go to the left for a second **screen**.	S'il-vous-plaît, dirigez vous à gauche pour une seconde **révision**.

Re-vee-seeon

Once past the security checks, it is time to find your gate.

Gate	Porte d'embarquement
Where is **gate** 15?	Où est la **porte d'embarquement** numéro 15?

Pohr-tuh dem-bahr-kuh-men

Flight	Vol
What **flight** are you taking?	Quel **vol** prenez-vous?

Boarding pass	Carte d'embarquement

www.LearnLikeNatives.com

| Please, have your **boarding pass** and passport in hand. | Veuillez avoir votre **carte d'embarquement** et votre passeport à proximité, s'il vous-plaît. |

Kar-tuh dem-bahr-kuh-men

| Seat | Siège |
| My **seat** is 23F. | Mon siege est le 23F. |

Sieh-guh

| Bathroom | Salle de bain |
| Is that **bathroom** occupied? | Est-ce que la **salle de bain** est occupée? |

Sal-duh-bein

| Blanket | Couverture |
| Can I have a **blanket**? | Puis-je avoir une **couverture**? |

Koo-ver-tur

You know, I could teach you how to ask for other stuff... like some wine? Which is "vin", but let's be responsible and learn some emergency signals.

Go through	Passer
I need to **go through**.	Je dois **passer**.

Pah-seh

Feeling sick	Se sentir malade
I am feeling **sick**.	Je me sens **malade**.

Mah-lah-duh

"Sick" translates directly as "malade". So, work on your phrasing, but especially remember that word, "ma-la-duh". Hearing "sick" in any language is a sign for help.

Headache	Mal de tête
I have a **headache**.	J'ai un **mal de tête**.

Mal duh tet

www.LearnLikeNatives.com

Fever	Fièvre
I have a **fever**.	J'ai de la **fièvre**.

Fee-eh-vruh

Nausea	Nausée
I feel **nauseous**.	Je me sens **nauséeux/nauséuse**. (if you're a woman)

No-zé-euh / No-zé-euh-zuh

Allergic	Allergique
I am **allergic** to…	Je suis **allergique** à…

Ah-ler-gee-kuh

Obviously, I really hope you won't need to use any of these words, but it's better to be prepared for even unpleasant situations.

www.LearnLikeNatives.com

What are your thoughts so far? Look at everything that we have just learned. Now you will be able to speak with the airport staff, catch a plane, enjoy a movie, and land safely. Join me for a little dialogue.

Flight Attendant: *Hello! Boarding pass, please.*

Bonjour! Carte d'embarquement, s'il-vous-plaît.

Cris: *Hello!*

Bonjour!

Flight Attendant: *Welcome! You're at seat 14F. By the window.*

Bienvenue! Votre siège est le 14F. Près de la fenêtre.

Cris: *Thanks!*

Merci!

Flight Attendant: *What would you like to drink today?*

Que voulez-vous boire?

Cris: *I would like some water with ice.*

J'aimerais avoir de l'eau avec des glaçons.

Flight Attendant:	*Of course! Anything else I can do for you?*
	Bien-sûr! Est-ce-que je peux faire autre chose pour vous?
Cris:	*Yes, I am actually feeling a little sick.*
	Oui, Je me sens un peu malade.
Flight Attendant:	*What are your symptoms?*
	Quels sont vos symptômes?
Cris:	*I have a headache and a slight fever.*
	J'ai mal à la tête et un peu de fièvre.
Flight Attendant:	*Are you allergic to something?*
	Etes-vous allergique à quelque chose?
Cris:	*Only to aspirin.*
	Seulement à l'aspirine.
Flight Attendant:	*Ok. Please let me get help.*
	D'accord. Permettez-moi d'aller chercher de l'aide.

Yes, I know what you are thinking. I have chosen the sick-person situation as an example. But how can you blame me? After all, I warned you that this book has been studied for you to feel confident in any situation! How is your head? Are you feeling any better? Not yet? Don't worry. We are landing now.

www.LearnLikeNatives.com

Chapter 3 – Looking for a Ride?

Welcome to the holiday you always dreamed about! There's just one more thing you will have to worry about before you can enjoy a refreshing drink next to the Eiffel Tower: how to get to your hotel. And so, the time has come to test your knowledge. Now that you arrived at your destination, your super-intensive-Italian immersion is about to start. How exciting is that?

First, let's begin with some basic words.

Taxi	Taxi
I need a **taxi**.	J'ai besoin d'un **taxi**.

Same word? 1 point for globalization!

Shuttle	Navette
Where can I get a **shuttle** to the Hilton Paris Opera?	Ou est-ce que je peux prendre la **navette** pour le Hilton Opera Paris?

Nav-veh-tuh

Bus	Bus
Where can I take a **bus** downtown?	Ou est-ce que je peux prendre un **bus** dans le centre?

Remember, the sound for the French "u" doesn't exist in English. The closest sound we have in English is OU as in "soup".

If you are traveling with family, you are possibly thinking about driving around. We should take you to a car rental.

Rent a car	Louer une voiture
I want to **rent a car**.	Je veux **louer une voiture**.

Vwa-tuu-ruh

Driver's license	Permis de conduire
I will need a **driver's license**.	J'aurai besoin d'un **permis de conduire**.

Per-mi duh con-dwi-ruh

www.LearnLikeNatives.com

You finally made it to your hotel. The panorama is wonderful and your room has a nice view all over Paris. Can you imagine it? Great! Me too! You will be able to get some rest soon. But, first, you have to check-in.

Check-in	Check in
I would like to **check into** my room.	J'aimerais faire le **check in** de ma chambre.

As you can see, check-in is used in French as well, and it's pronounced in the same way.

Reservation	Réservation
Under what name is the reservation?	Sous quel nom est la **réservation?**

Reh-zer-vah-ssion

Key	Clef
Here is your **key**.	Voici votre **clef**.

Klé (Here, you don't pronounce the "f".)

This is going to depend on what type of hotel you stay in. They now have keycards (clefs magnétiques), or you can even access by pin code (code). In any case, you can use the general word "clef", and everyone will understand.

Elevator	Ascenseur
The **elevator** is down the hall.	L' **ascenseur** se trouve au bout du couloir.

ah-sen-seur

Floor	Etage
Our room is on the 7th **floor.**	Notre chambre se trouve au 7ème **étage**.

This one sounds like "é-ta-guh".

Hey! I know you are eager to get into your room, so let's go in. Hey! I know you can't wait to see your room, so come on, open the door!
Look around your room. I am sure there is a nice comfy bed, maybe a flat-screen, and a closet. You stop a minute to admire

the sunset from your window. But now it's time to learn the name of the things around you.

Bed	Lit
Honey! Our **bed** is huge!	Chéri! Notre **lit** est énorme!

Once again, the "t" doesn't pronounce itself. "lee"

TV	Télévision/ TV
Is it a smart **TV**?	Est-ce-qu'il s'agit d'une smart **TV**?

Closet	Armoire
I'll put the suitcases in the **closet**.	Je vais mettre les valises dans l'**armoire**.

Ar-mwah-ruh.

Go inside your bathroom. Given that bathrooms go with water, and water leaks, you want to pay attention to the following words and phrases in case you have to report any problems with the pipes.

Shower	Douche
We have a massage **shower**.	Nous avons une **douche** hydromassante.

Doo-shuh. I know what you are thinking, this sounds like another word I know. Keep in mind that in French, the "ch" sound is similar to the "sh" one.

Toilet	Toilettes
Two bathrooms! We have a **toilet** each.	Deux salles-de-bains! Nous avons chacun nos **toilettes**.

Twa-let

Sink	Lavabo
I will put some things by the **sink**.	Je vais mettre des affaires à côté du **lavabo**.

La-va-boh

Towels	Serviettes

Hello! I need more **towels**.	Bonjour! J'aurais besoin de plus de **serviettes**.

Ser-vee-et

Pillows	Coussins
I also need 2 more **pillows**.	J'aurais aussi besoin de deux **coussins** de plus.

Koo-sen

It turns out my girlfriend uses four pillows, and I always use extra towels. These two are basic survival for us.

Also, some hotels don't put mini-fridges inside the bedrooms anymore. In case you have any requests, follow me to the next phrase.

Mini fridge	Mini-réfrigirateur
I would like a **mini-fridge** in my bedroom.	J'aimerais avoir un **mini-réfrigérateur** dans ma chambre.

You know the word for "mini". Let's practice the hard one:

Ré-fri-ge-ra-tuhr
Mini-réfrigérateur

You have a nice bedroom in there! So, how about some practice?

Concierge: *Hello! How can I help you?*

Bonjour! Comment puis-je vous aider?

Dan: *Hello! I think my sink is leaking.*

Bonjour! Je pense que mon lavabo coule.

Concierge: *I will send someone right away!*

Je vais vous envoyer quelqu'un tout de suite!

Dan: *Thanks. I appreciate your help.*

Merci pour votre aide.

Concierge: *I am sorry for the inconvenience. Is there anything I can do to make your stay more pleasant?*

Je suis désolé pour le désagrément. Est-ce que je peux faire quelque chose pour rendre votre séjour plus agréable?

www.LearnLikeNatives.com

Dan: *Now that you mention it, I notice my room does not have a mini-fridge.*

Maintenant que vous le mentionnez, je vois qu'il n'y a pas de mini-réfrigérateur dans ma chambre.

Concierge: *Of course! Anything else?*

Bien-sûr, je m'en occupe. Autre chose?

Dan: *I'd like a couple more towels, and one extra pillow, please.*

J'aimerais avoir deux serviettes supplémentaires, et un coussin, s'il vous plait.

Concierge: *Sure! Just in case you need more pillows, you have an extra inside the closet.*

Bien-sûr! Juste au cas ou, si vous avez besoin de coussins supplémentaires, vous en avez un dans l'armoire.

Dan: *Good to know! Thanks!*

C'est bon à savoir! Merci!

Concierge: *Is there anything else I can do for you today?*

Est-ce que je peux faire autre chose pour vous?

Dan: *I am okay. Thank you very much.*

Non tout vas bien. Merci beaucoup.

Concierge: *I will send all that right away. Again, sorry for the inconvenience.*

Je vous envoie tout ça immédiatement. Encore une fois, navré pour le désagrément.

Dan: *It is all good. Thanks for your help.*

C'est tout bon. Merci pour votre aide.

Concierge: *Thank you for being our guest!*

Merci à vous, d'être notre client!

Good! I think we are all set! Ready to go work on your tan?

www.LearnLikeNatives.com

Chapter 4 – I Find My Happiness Where the Sun Shines

You are finally here, where you have always dreamed to be. The weather is wonderful, and the sounds of church bells ringing are amplified in your room. A small orchestra is playing in the distance. This is all you ever wanted, and now you are ready to go out and discover everything that this amazing place has to offer.

Before heading out, let's check the weather.

Weather	Climat
How's the **weather** in Paris?	Comment est le **climat** à Paris?

Klee-mah

First, just a quick check-up on the seasons.

Spring	Printemps

| Flowers are blooming. **Spring** is here. | Les fleurs fleurissent. C'est le **printemps.** |

Pren-tam

Summer	été
In the tropics, it always feels like **summer**.	Dans les tropiques, on se sent toujours en **été**.

é-té

Fall	Automne
Look at the trees, and their **fall** colors.	Regardez les arbres, et leurs couleurs **d'automne**.

Oh-toh-nuh

As you know, the weather can change quickly. Generally, summer is hot and dry, while winter is cold, but sometimes the weather can change many times a day.

| Cloud | Nuage |

| Look at that big **cloud**. | Regardez ce gros **nuage.** |

Nu-ah-guh

| Sun | Soleil |

| The **sun** was too strong. | Le **soleil** tappait trop fort. |

So-ley

| Rain | Pluie |

| The **rain** came without a warning. | La **pluie** est arrivée d'un coup. |

Plu-ee

| Storm | Tempête |

| Before we knew, the **storm** was here. | Avant même de réaliser, la **tempête** était là. |

Is there any popular movie you can think of? I can remember quite a few.

| Wind | Vent |

The **wind** was so strong that the windows were moving.	Le **vent** était tellement fort que les fenêtres bougeaient.

Degrees	Degrés
It was under 0 **degrees**.	Il faisait moins de 0 **degrés**.

Duh-gré

Something to keep in mind is that the metric system is common outside the US. Depending on your destination, having a unit converter could be very useful.

Hurricane	Ouragan
The **hurricane** wrecked it all.	L'**ouragan** a tout détruit.

Ooh-rah-guan. It's the perfect word to practice your "r" sound with.

Sunglasses	Lunettes de soleil

I left my **sunglasses** on the bed!	J'ai laissé mes **lunettes de soleil** sur le lit!

Lu-né-tuh de so-ley

Hat	Châpeau
That's a nice **hat**!	Ce **châpeau** est sympa!

Sha-poh

Sunscreen	Crème solaire
Did you bring **sunscreen**?	As-tu amené de la **crème solaire**?

Crem soh-ler

Umbrella	Parapluie
Let's get under that **umbrella**.	Allons en dessous de ce **parapluie**.

pah-rah-pluee

Raincoat	Imperméable

It is necessary to bring your **raincoat**.	C'est indispensable d'emmener son **imperméable**.

In-per-meh-ah-bluh

This is a very useful word. It is used to indicate a raincoat or just to indicate that something is waterproof: "Impermeabile". Keep it in mind! You may want to get one next time you go shopping.

Talking about shopping, why don't we go for a little spree?

Seller: *Hello! Good afternoon. How can I help you?*

Bonjour! Comment puis-je vous aider?

Ken: *Hey! Good afternoon. I would like to buy some things.*

Bonjour! J'aimerais acheter plusieures choses.

Seller: *Sure! What do you have in mind?*

Bien-sûr! Qu'avez-vous en tête?

Ken: *Everything. I need an umbrella, sunglasses, a raincoat... everything.*

	Tout. J'ai besoin d'un parapluie, de lunettes de soleil, d'un imperméable… tout.
Seller:	*Oh, I see. Did the hurricane catch you off guard?*
	Oh, je vois. Vous avez été surprise par l'ouragan?
Ken:	*Yes. Totally. It's been crazy. Sun goes, and rain comes. Repeatedly.*
	Oui, totalement. C'est dingue. Le soleil part, la pluie arrive. Constamment.
Seller:	*I am sorry to hear that. I will help you gladly.*
	Je suis désolé de l'entendre. C'est mon plaisir de vous assister.
Ken:	*Thanks! What raincoats do you have?*
	Merci! Vous avez quoi comme imperméables?
Seller:	*I have these raincoats. Good quality and they protect you down to 0 degrees.*
	J'ai ceux-ci. Ils sont de bonne qualité et vous protègent jusqu'à 0 degrés.
Ken:	*Awesome! What about umbrellas?*

Super! Qu'en-est-il des parapluies?

Seller: *I have many. It depends on what size you are looking for.*

J'en ai beaucoup. Cela dépend de quelle taille vous recherchez.

Ken: *Just a couple of small umbrellas. Something easy to carry.*

Juste deux petits parapluies. Quelque chose de facile à porter.

Seller: *Sure! Why don't you come with me to pick sunglasses?*

D'accord! Vous voulez venir avec moi pour choisir des lunettes de soleil?

Ken: *Glad to! I will follow you.*

Avec Plaisir! Je vous suis.

Seller: *Very well. This way, please.*

Très bien. Par ici, s'il-vous-plaît.

I hope you have sunscreen. The rain is finally gone, so we are going to some touristy places in a little while and I do not want you to get a nasty sunburn. Remember to bring all your equipment. As always, the most important thing is to be prepared.

Chapter 5 – I Have So Many Stories to Tell You

Do you know what I love most about life in general? The stories! And this is especially true for traveling, because it is all about learning new cultures, meeting new and different people, and facing things you never thought you would.

I remember being in this beautiful sunny place in a little old town in the south of France, not far from the Spanish border. Everything looked perfect. The location was terrific; it was close to everything I needed, and the architecture in our hotel was breathtakingly beautiful. The price was good. Everything was perfect… until I got to my room and found out my toilet was inside the shower.

Trust me, I am not picky. I decided to stay there for the night because the location was amazing and the hotel had already been paid for. I have to admit, though, that all optimism vanished after I went to the bathroom in the middle of the night and got my socks wet from the shower. Needless to say, it was a GREAT and funny story to tell my friends and one of those things I will remember forever.

If you are a storyteller, as I am, then you need a few more tools so you can delight your friends–even your newest local friends–with the fantastic things you have gone through. For that, we will use two different verbal forms to help you bring your story to life. You know this, or at least you may have heard of it back in school. Don't worry. We promised no grammar, okay? I want to show you some examples.

First, let's go through the first one: past simple, which in French, we call "passé simple".

However, the passé simple isn't used often anymore. Therefore, the more appropriate one would be the "passé composé" meaning the composed past.

Why "composed"? Because it is composed of "avoir" (to have) or "être" (to be) + the main verb.

Here, you have to conjugate only "to be" or "to have", while the termination of the main verb remains the same. Easy, right?

Let me explain: The past participle is formed by adding the following endings to the verb stem:

- *é* for verbs ending in *-er*
- *i* for the majority of verbs ending in *-ir*

- *u* with verbs like *attendre, boire, voir, lire*, etc.
- *it* or *is* with verbs like *écrire, dire, prendre*, etc.

The past participle is used to form compound tenses (*passé composé, plus-que-parfait, passif,* etc) with the auxiliary verbs *être* and *avoir*.

We'll start with a verb we know, "voyager"- to travel. Remember how we conjugate the verb "avoir" - "to have". This will give you the opportunity to revise it, in case you have forgotten it.

The participle passé always remains the same.

To travel	Voyager	Root	Termination
I traveled	J'ai voyagé	Voyag-	Er changes to "é"
You traveled	Tu as voyagé		Er changes to "é"
He/She/ traveled	Il/elle a voyagé		Er changes to "é"
We traveled	Nous avons voyagé		Er changes to "é"
You traveled	Vous avez voyagé		Er changes to "é"

They traveled	Ils/elles ont voyagé		Er changes to "é"

See? It's not that difficult right? You just need to remember the conjugation of "Avoir", and then the verb remains the same!

Let's go for a quick practice.

I traveled to France last year.	J'ai voyagé en France l'année dernière.
She traveled through the entire continent.	Ella a voyagé à travers tout le continent.
You traveled a lot the last two months.	Tu as beaucoup voyagé les deux derniers mois.
We traveled to Mexico during the summer.	Nous avons voyagé au Mexique durant l'été.

Can you see? In every sentence, all the actions have already happened: last year, last summer, the last two months.

www.LearnLikeNatives.com

To eat	Manger	Root	Termination
I ate	J'ai mangé	Mang-	Er changes to "é"
You ate	Tu as mangé		Er changes to "é"
He/She ate	Il/Elle a mangé		Er changes to "é"
We ate	Nous avons mangé		Er changes to "é"
You ate	Vous avez mangé		Er changes to "é"
They ate	Ils ont mangé		Er changes to "é"

Let's practice with some sentences.

You ate the entire cake.	Tu as mangé le gâteau en entier.
She ate only a piece of cake.	Elle a mangé seulement un morceau du gâteau.

We ate one piece each.	Nous avons mangé un morceau chacun.
They ate the rest of the cake.	Ils ont mangé le reste du gâteau.

This is important for stories–everyone has to eat! Also, as seen, it is a good verb to help solve some family culinary disputes.

Same goes for verbs with the "ir" termination, such as "finir":

To finish	**Finir**	**Root**	**Termination**
I finished	J'ai fini		Ir changes to "i"
You finished	Tu as fini		Ir changes to "i"
He/She finished	Il/Elle a fini		Ir changes to "i"
We finished	Nous avons fini	Fin-	Ir changes to "i"
You finished	Vous avez fini		Ir changes to "i"
They finished	Ils/Elles ont fini		Ir changes to "i"

Are you getting closer? Let's go for some practice.

You finished your homework.	Tu as fini tes devoirs.
He finished his shift.	Il a fini son service.
They finished cooking dinner.	Ils ont fini de cuisiner le repas du soir.

As we discussed earlier, for all regular verbs ending in "er" and "ir", you only have to conjugate the verb "Avoir" (to have) followed by the verb you want to use. Find the root of the verb and then add the same termination each time.

How are you doing so far? Don't worry. We will keep working on this a little longer, using more examples.

Irregular past participles

Here you have a list of the most common verbs with irregular past particple. Memorize them, and you'll make your life with verbs so much easier.

English Verb	**French Verb**	**Past participle**
To can	**pouvoir**	pu
To want	**vouloir**	voulu

To have to /must	devoir	dû
To open	ouvrir	ouvert
To suffer	souffrir	souffert
To drive	conduire	Conduit
To build	construire	construit
To produce	produire	produit
To receive	Recevoir	reçu
To hold	Tenir	tenu
To believe	croire	cru
To lose	perdre	perdu

As with any other language, French is all about structure, and I promise it will get easier with some practice. As always, I will point other practical uses for this tense through the dialogue.

Undefined past

On the other side, in sentences using the imperfect past (passé imparfait), you never know when the action started or ended. It's the equivalent to say that "you used to" do something. You know it's not happening anymore, but can't really tell when it ended. With this being said, let's see some examples using the same verbs as before.

To travel	Voyager	Root	Termination
I traveled	Je voyageais	Voyag-	Er changes to "eais"
You traveled	Tu voyageais		Er changes to "eais"
He/She/It traveled	Il/Elle voyageait		Er changes to "eait"
We traveled	Nous voyagions		Er changes to "ions"
You traveled	Vous voyagiez		Er changes to "iez"
They traveled	Ils/Elles voyageaient		Er changes to "eaient"

Do you see what we did there? For conjugating regular verbs, you need to spot the root of the verb and then shift the termination, according to each case. For the verb "voyager", the root is "voyag-". For the verb "aimer" (to like), the root is "aim-". And for the verb "former" (to form), we have to employ the root "form-".

The same thing will happen for most of the verbs ending in "er", as in "manger" (root "mang-") or "chanter" (root "chant-"), and for the "ir" termination group, as in partir" (root "par-") or "réléchir" (root "réfléch-").

Come on! It may look hard, but it is not really that awful. You just need some practice and a few pointers, like the ones we discussed.

I traveled all the time, until I lost my passport.	Je voyageais tout le temps, jusqu'à ce que je perde mon passeport.
She traveled the continent while he was getting his degree.	Elle voyageait à travers le continent pendant qu'il passait son diplôme.
You traveled before having kids.	Vous voyagiez avant d'avoir des enfants.
We traveled every two months.	Nous voyagions tous les deux mois.

www.LearnLikeNatives.com

Notice how in these last sentences, you could have used "used to travel" instead of "traveled". This is important because it works as a hint–every time you can change an English verb in the past tense for a "used to + verb", you are in the presence of French imperfect past, and therefore all changes apply as we just practiced.

I used to travel all the time until I lost my passport.	Je voyageais tout le temps, jusqu'à ce que je perde mon passeport.
She used to travel the continent, while he was getting his degree.	Elle voyageait à travers le continent pendant qu'il passait son diplôme.
You used to travel before having kids.	Vous voyagiez avant d'avoir des enfants.
We used to travel every two months.	Nous voyagions tous les deux mois.

Are you getting better with your phrasing? Let's keep working.

| To eat | Manger | Root | Termination |

I ate	Je mangeais	Mang-	Er changes to "eais"
You ate	Tu mangeais		Er changes to "eais"
He/She ate	Il/Elle mangeait		Er changes to "eait"
We ate	Nous mangions		Er changes to "ions"
You ate	Vous mangiez		Er changes to "iez"
They ate	Ils mangeaient		Er changes to "eaient"

As always, don't worry. Practice makes perfect and in no time, you will have each tense covered. Let's keep practicing.

You ate an entire cake while I was watching TV.	Tu mangeais un gâteau en entier pendant que je regardais la télé.
She ate one piece of cake after dinner every night.	Elle mangeait un morceau de gâteau tous les soirs après le diner.

We ate one piece every time we saw each other.	Nous en mangions à chaque fois qu'on se voyait.
That night, they ate with so much joy!	Cette nuit-là, ils mangeaient avec tant de joie !

How is this sounding to you? Is it making any sense? Let's see more verbs.

To discover	Descubrir	Root	Termination
I discovered	Je découvrais	Decouvr-	Ir changes to "ais"
You discovered	Tu découvrais		Ir changes to "ais"
He/She/ discovered	Il/Elle découvrait		Ir changes to "ait"
We discovered	Nous découvrions		Ir changes to "ions"
You discovered	Vous découvriez		Ir changes to "iez"
They discovered	Ils/Elles découvraient		Ir changes to "aient"

Can you see how the terminations shift? Let's see some examples.

I discovered new ways before that happened.	Je découvrais de nouvelles façons, avant que cela n'arrive.
You discovered new ways to surprise me, night after night.	Tu découvrais de nouvelles façons de me surprendre, nuit après nuit.
She discovered a mark, and then another.	Elle découvrait une tâche, puis une autre.
They discovered what happened, until you found out.	Ils découvraient ce qui s'était passé, jusqu'à ce que tu l'apprennes.

See? It can get easier, quick. Let's go to our next verb: the irregular "to have", or "Avoir".

To have	**Avoir**
I had	J'avais
You had	Tu avais
He/She had	Il/Elle avait
We had	Nous avions
You had	Vous aviez

| They had | Ils/Elles avaient |

I had everything I could wish for.	J'avais tout ce que je désirais.
She had every opportunity.	Elle avait toutes les opportunités.
You had other plans, and it worked.	Tu avais d'autres plans et ça marchait.
We had so much to do.	Nous avions tellement de choses à faire.

Pay attention to the next verb. The verb "to be" is also an option when building sentences that are more complex. This turns it into a necessary tool to have in order to tell a great story.

To be	**être**
I was	J'étais
You were	Tu étais
He/She was	Il/Elle était

www.LearnLikeNatives.com

We were	Nous étions
You were	Vous étiez
They were	Ils/Elles étaient

Let's practice a bit more.

I was a Prom Queen.	J'étais la reine du bal.
He was a great athlete.	Il était un grand athlète.
We were a great team.	Nous étions une équipe formidable.
They were invincible.	Ils étaient invincibles.

After all those "different" pasts, you might be a little confused. Don't worry, I am going to present you two verbal forms that will save your life! Those require little to no conjugation and will allow you to express yourself in the most common situations.

1. Le présent progressif - the present progressive

It could be compared to the present continuous in English. It forms with the verb to be in the present and the expression "in train from/to" + verb to infinitive.

Examples:

What are you doing? I'm working.	Tu fais quoi ? Je suis en train de travailler.
Have you finished writing the letter? We are finishing.	Tu as fini d'écrire la lettre ? Nous sommes en train de finir.
Did he go to the grocery store? He is shopping right now.	Est-il allé au supermarché? Il est en train de faire les courses maintenant.
They are taking a test in classroom A.	Ils sont en train de passer une évaluation dans la salle A.

2. Le passé récent - The recent past

To express an action in the past that is close to the moment we speak, we use the verb « venir » in the present + de/d* + verb without conjugation.

At this time, I am sure that you already know how to conjugate the verb « venir » at the present tense, but just in case, here you have it once again.

Examples :

I just phoned my mother	Je viens d'appeler ma mère.
You have just arrived	Tu viens d'arriver.
He just arrived at the party.	Il vient d'arriver à la fête.
We just had dinner.	Nous venons de dîner.
The train has just left.	Le train vient de partir.

Through our dialogue, you will have the chance to see how all these elements fit together.

Kate: *Hello! I am so glad you came back from your trip. When did you arrive?*

Salut! Je suis tellement contente que tu sois revenue de ton voyage. Quand es-tu arrivé?

Alex: *Hi! I am glad as well. It was a fun trip. I've just arrived.*

Salut! Moi aussi. C'était un voyage sympathique. Je viens d'arriver.

Kate: *Great! Tell me!*

Super! Racontes-moi!

Alex: *Remember how I used to love rain?*

Tu te rappelles comme j'aimais la pluie?

Kate: *Of course.*

Bien-sûr.

Alex: *It turns out it was raining in Paris, but I had bought tickets to see a movie.*

Il s'est avéré qu'il pleuvait à Paris, mais j'avais acheté des billets pour aller regarder un film.

Kate: *Such a pity!*

C'est dommage!

Alex: *I have always had that thing with rain.*

J'ai toujours eu cette malchance avec la pluie.

Kate: *Indeed.*

Effectivement.

Alex: *It's fine, I still managed to visit a lot of places. The front desk agent gave me an umbrella.*

Ça va, j'ai quand même pu visiter beaucoup d'endroits. Le réceptionniste m'a donné un parapluie.

Kate: *Oh, that's nice!*

Oh, c'est gentil!

Alex: *You would love Paris, the food was delicious, I would love to go back.*

Tu adorerais Paris, la nourriture était délicieuse. J'adorerais y retourner.

Kate: *I've always wanted to go. We should plan a trip together!*

J'ai toujours voulue y aller. Nous devrions plannifier un voyage ensemble!

Alex: *Definitely! Have you finished your workday? We could grab a coffee and talk more.*

Certainement! Tu as fini ta journée de travail? On pourrait prendre un café et en parler.

Kate: *I am finishing one thing, but I can meet you in 5 minutes!*

Je suis en train de finir quelque chose mais je peux te rejoindre dans 5 minutes!

Alex: *Awesome! I will wait for you here.*

Super! Je t'attendrai ici.

Do you feel like an expert at putting phrases together? You should. We have come a long way. Besides, you are going to need those skills now because we are going on an adventure.

Chapter 6 – So Many Roads and So Many Places

I personally love to walk. When I was younger and single, I would put my earphones in and walk through any new city I got the chance to visit. Now, with my girlfriend, I put the headphones away and we enjoy long chats while walking and looking around. Sometimes she takes pictures, and they are mostly of me taking pictures of her or the landscape. But I enjoy watching her under all the different shades and lights. Have you ever noticed how every city has different colors and vibes?

Back to business. Tell me, what do you typically want to visit first when exploring a new city? Wherever you want to go, I am here to help you. Why don't we start with a few basics?

Museum	Musée
Where is the Louvres **Museum**?	Où se trouve le **musée** du Louvres?

Mu-zé

Square	Place
How can I get to Saint-Georges **Square**?	Comment puis-je me rendre à la **place** Saint-Georges?

Pla-ssuh

Avenue	Avenue
What can I find on the main **avenue?**	Que puis-je trouver sur l'**avenue** principale?

Ah-veh-nuh

This one should not be a problem. The pronunciation is very similar to the English "avenue".

Monuments	Monuments
Paris is rich in history and **monuments.**	Paris est riche en histoire et **monuments.**

Moh-nuh-men

Park	Parc
Park Buttes-Chaumont is in Paris.	Le **Parc** Buttes-Chaumont se situe à Paris.

Par-k

Church	Eglise
They gave me this **church** as a reference.	Ils m'ont donné cette **église** comme référence.

Ee-glee-zuh

Not to be disrespectful, but travelling is not just about history and monuments. It is also about having fun and experiencing the true local culture, as well as going to bars and clubs.

Bar	Bar
Where is this **bar**?	Où se trouve ce **bar**?

See? Globalization scores again!

Now that you have learned the name of some places, let's go there together.

Across	En face
You can find them **across** the avenue.	Vous pouvez les trouver **en face** de l'avenue.

En fah-suh

In front of	Devant

| He is waiting **in front of** the statue. | Il attends **devant** la statue. |

Deh-van

| Opposite | Opposé |

| We were walking in the **opposite** direction. | Nous étions en train de marcher du côté **opposé**. |

Oh-poo-zé

| Street | Rue |

| You can find it down the **street**. | Vous pouvez trouver ça en bas de la **rue**. |

ruh

| Subway | Métro |

| We can get there by **subway**. | Nous pouvons nous y rendre en **métro**. |

Meh-troh – This word comes from "Metropolitain" which as you can guess, means "Metropolitan".

| Mall | Centre commercial |

| What kind of **mall** would you like to visit? | Quel type de **centre commercial** souhaiteriez-vous visiter? |

Cen-truh ko-mer-sial

Recommend	Recommander
What can you **recommend?**	Qu'est-ce que vous **recommandez?**

Re-co-men-déh

"Recommander" is a general word for "suggestions". So, whenever you are out of ideas, just remember this one.

In terms of tourism, you should already be an expert at getting around. You learned how to request a cab, rent a car, and ask for directions and recommendations. You are almost done with this section, so why don't we practice a little more?

Front desk (Recepción):	*Hello! How can I help you?*
	Bonjour! Comment puis-je vous aider?
Allen:	*I would like some recommendations for places to visit.*

	J'aimerais avoir des recommandations d'endroits à visiter.
Front desk:	*Very well. What type of place did you have in mind? A club, a museum?*
	Très bien. Quel type d'endroit aviez-vous en tête ? Un club, un musée ?
Allen:	*I heard that you have beautiful squares and monuments in this city.*
	J'ai entendu que vous avez des places et des monuments magnifiques dans la ville.
Front desk:	*That is true. Sadly, most cultural attractions are across town.*
	C'est vrai. Malheureusement, la plupart des attractions touristiques sont de l'autre côté de la ville.
Philip:	*Oh, I see. Could you give me some directions, please?*
	Oh, je vois. Pouvez-vous m'indiquer comment m'y rendre, s'il-vous-plaît ?

Front desk: *Sure! Would you like to travel by car or take the subway?*

Bien-sûr ! Vous préferez vous y rendre en voiture ou plutôt prendre le métro ?

Philip: *I would rather take a subway and walk.*

Je préfèrerais prendre le métro et marcher.

Front desk: *Very well. The subway is only 300m away.*

Très bien. Le métro se trouve à seulement 300m d'ici.

Philip: *Perfect! How do I get there?*

Parfait ! Comment puis-je m'y rendre ?

Front desk: *You only have to go down this street, take a right, and walk straight for 200m.*

Vous avez seulement à descendre la rue, prendre à droite puis marcher tout droit pendant 200m.

Philip: *That sounds easy. Thank you very much!*

	Ça à l'air facile. Merci beaucoup!
Front desk:	*All right, then. After you get to the subway, go to the mainline and take a train to étoile station.*
	D'accord, alors, en arrivant au métro, allez à la ligne principale et prenez le métro jusqu'à la station étoile.
Philip:	*Very good. I appreciate your help.*
	Très bien. Merci pour votre aide.
Front desk:	*My pleasure. Have a nice day.*
	Avec Plaisir. Bonne journée.
Allen:	*Likewise. Bye.*
	Egalement. Au revoir.

Ready to walk around the city and get lost in its little streets? I'm sure you can't wait. Then you'd better get ready. Go out and have fun. Who knows how many funny stories you will be able to tell once back from your trip!

Although now I am getting a bit hungry. Sorry, what did you say? Should we go and grab a bite to eat?

Chapter 7 – Eat, Travel, Love

Food is one of my favorite parts of traveling. Eating is an awesome way to learn a bit more about the culture and history of each place. Your nose and tongue become guides that can lead you through unknown passages, allowing you to enjoy the aromas of France in a glass of Cabernet; or to experience the culinary revolution in Paris, in the shape of a sweet and crusty croissant. Flavors are unique everywhere you go, and that is what makes them a huge part of traveling.

For this reason, I want to be sure I am giving you the opportunity to have the best experience. Plus, ordering food is a recurrent activity, which means you will have many chances to practice. I can also assure you something: some of the best typical food places will not have a translator. With that in mind, let's start this chapter.

Restaurant	Restaurant
Let's go into that **restaurant.**	Rentrons dans ce **restaurant.**

Rehs-to-ran

It is very similar to the English word, except for the intonation (Also, French people don't pronounce the "t" at the end.)

Table	Table
Table for four, please.	Une **table** pour quatre, s'il-vous-plaît.

Once again, the word is the same but the pronunciation is not. The French way to pronounce is: Tah-bluh".

Suggestions	Suggestions
Do you want to hear today's **suggestions?**	Vous voulez voir les **suggestions** du jour?

Suh-gest-eeon

Portion	Portion
I want a **portion** of fries.	J'aimerais avoir une **portion** de frites.

Pors-eeon

Quite easy, huh?

Fork	Fourchette
I dropped my **fork.**	J'ai fait tomber ma **fourchette.**

Foor-chett

www.LearnLikeNatives.com

Spoon	Cuillère
Can I get a **spoon**?	Puis-je avoir une **cuillère**?

Cu-ee-eh-ruh

Knife	Couteau
I will need a meat **knife**.	J'aurais besoin d'un **couteau** à viande.

Koo-toh

Plate	Assiette
Can you bring an extra **plate**?	Pouvez-vous apporter une **assiette** en plus?

Ass-ee-et

Entry	Entrée
Do you want an **entry**?	Voulez-vous une **entrée**?

An-tré

Main dish	Plat principal
For the **main dish**, I want the chicken.	En **plat principal**, j'aimerais le poulet.

Pla-prehn-si-pal

Well-cooked	Bien cuit
I want my steak **well-cooked.**	J'aimerais mon steak **bien cuit.**

Bee-n   koo-ee

"Bien" (Bee-n) means "good".

Medium	A point
Medium is fine for me.	**A point,** ça me convient.

Ah poo-ehn

Dessert	Dessert
Of course, I want a **dessert.**	Bien-sûr que j'aimerais avoir un **dessert.**

Deh-ssehr (The "s" is pronounced as "s", not as a "z", like the English way.)

Vegan	Végétalien
Do you have a vegan menu?	Est-ce que vous avez un menu **végétalien?**

Veh-geh-tal-ee-ehn (Note that French people also say "vegan" sometimes, so they will probably understand this word, especially in restaurants.)

Check	Addition
I want the **check**, please.	J'aimerais avoir l'**addition**, s'il-vous-plaît.

Ah-dee-ssion

Are you excited to order your first dish? Why don't we go practice a bit more first…

Waiter (serveur): *Good afternoon! Welcome to our restaurant. My name is Shawn. How many are you?*

Bonjour! Bienvenue dans notre restaurant. Mon nom est Shawn. Vous êtes combien?

Mike: *Hello! We have a reservation under Paulson. Table for four.*

Bonjour! Nous avons une réservation sous le nom de Paulson, table pour quatre.

Waiter: *Yes, here you are. Come with me, please.*

Oui, je vois. Venez avec moi, s'il-vous-plaît.

Mike: *I would like to order right away. We are starving.*

J'aimerais commander maintenant. Nous sommes morts de faim.

Waiter: *Perfect. What would you like to order?*

Parfait. Que voulez-vous commander?

Mike: *What are your suggestions?*

Quelles sont vos suggestions?

Waiter: *The lobster ceviche as an appetizer. For the main dish, we have a beef tartare which is excellent.*

Le ceviche de homard en entrée. En plat principal, nous avons un excellent tartare de boeuf.

Mike: *Sounds great! I want one of each. Also, a salad and two beef dishes.*

Ça a l'air fabuleux! Je voudrais un de chaque. Aussi, une salade et deux plats à base de boeuf.

Waiter:	*Do you want extra plates to share?*	
	Vous voulez des assiettes pour partager?	
Mike:	*Yes, please.*	
	Oui, s'il-vous-plaît.	
Waiter:	*Perfect. I will be back in a second with your plates, forks, and meat knives.*	
	Parfait. Je reviens dans une seconde avec vos assiettes, fourchettes et couteaux à viande.	
Mike:	*Thank you very much.*	
	Merci beaucoup.	
Waiter:	*I'll be right back.*	
	Je reviens tout de suite.	

I bet this chapter was easy. How did you feel after repeating that last dialogue? Look... I do not want to freak you out, but you are about to feel a bit under the weather.

www.LearnLikeNatives.com

Chapter 8 – Sick & Abroad!

Every time I travel abroad, I buy insurance, but the truth is I always hope I will not need it. Being sick can be scary, and no one likes to feel ill. Moreover, nobody wants it to interrupt their vacation! However, if you have to be prepared for something, this is definitely it. Great communication can be the key to solving major problems. So, let's get prepared.

Ill	Malade
I think I am **ill.**	Je crois que je suis **malade.**

Here we see the word "ma-lah-duh" again, I know, but it is very important.

Cold	Rhume
I think I caught a **cold.**	Je crois que j'ai attrapé un **Rhume.**

Ru-muh

Cough	Toux
I have a slight **cough.**	J'ai une petite **toux.**

Too

Pain	Douleur
I took something for the **pain**.	J'ai pris quelque chose pour la **douleur**.

Doo-leur

Migraine	Migraine
I have a **migraine**.	J'ai une **migraine**.

Mee-greh-nuh

Swollen	Gonflé
My throat is a bit **swollen**.	Ma gorge est un peu **gonflée**.

Gonf-leh

Call the doctor	Appeler le docteur
Do you want to call the **doctor**?	Est-ce que tu veux appeler le **docteur**?

Doc-tuhr

Emergency	Urgence
I have an **emergency**.	J'ai une **urgence**.

Ur-gen-ssuh

Feel	Sentir
I **feel** a bit better.	Je me **sens** un peu mieux.

Sen-teer

Patient	Patient
I am a **patient** of Dr. Castillo.	Je suis un **patient** du Dr. Castillo.

Pah-See-an

Blood pressure	Pression sanguine
The **blood pressure** is fine.	La **pression sanguine** est bien.

Preh-si-on san-ghee-nuh

Pharmacy	Pharmacie
Where is the nearest **pharmacy**?	Où est la **pharmacie** la plus proche?

Similar to English: "phar-ma-cee".

Prescription	Ordonnance

www.LearnLikeNatives.com

I will need a **prescription.**	Je vais avoir besoin d'une **ordonnance.**

Or-doh-naan-suh

Pills	Comprimés
How many **pills** do I need?	Il me faut combien de **comprimés**?

Com-pree-mé

We have already seen a similar scenario in a previous chapter, do you remember? So, this should be easy as we have covered it before. Are you ready to practice?

Liam: *Hello! I would like to speak to Dr. Castil.*

Bonjour! J'aimerais parler au Dr. Castil.

Secretary (secretaire): *Good afternoon, Sir. What is your name?*

Bonjour, monsieur. Puis-je avoir votre nom?

Liam: *I am Liam Smith. One of his patients.*

Je suis Liam Smith. Un de ses patients.

Secretary:	*Good afternoon, sir. Why do you call today?*
	Bonjour, monsieur. Quelle est la raison de votre appel?
Liam:	*I have an emergency. My youngest son has a strong headache.*
	J'ai une urgence. Mon plus jeune fils a un gros mal de tête.
Secretary:	*Any other symptoms?*
	D'autres symptomes?
Liam:	*38°C fever. Also complaints of abdominal pain.*
	38°C de fièvre. Il se plaint de douleurs abdominales.
Secretary:	*Is he allergic to something?*
	Est-ce qu'il est allergique à quelque chose?
Liam:	*Yes. To gluten.*
	Oui. Au gluten.

Secretary:	*Is he taking any prescriptions?*
	Est-ce qu'il prends un traitement?
Liam:	*No, just a dietary supplement.*
	Non. Juste des complements alimentaires.
Secretary:	*Come here at once and bring those pills.*
	Venez ici au plus vite et prenez les comprimés.

Yeah, I know what you are thinking: no parent with a celiac kid would give him random pills! I feel you, but I have also seen it happen.

I sincerely hope this book will help you better understand and speak French. I love to travel and the diversity in people and styles, and I hope you enjoy the same things. I know how much independence and confidence you can gain by being able to communicate in more than one language. So, stay with me! We need you focused! Did I forget to mention something? You are now looking for a job.

Chapter 9 – Learn the Ropes

Looking for new employment can be both a frustrating and an exciting situation. I am used to working on my own–which allows me to travel more–but I still have to get my own clients. If you are relocating or just thinking of spending a season in another city, finding a job at a local business could be a great opportunity to get in touch with the culture from a closer perspective.

As always, I will try to keep it simple.

Employment	Emploi
I am looking for **employment.**	Je cherche un **emploi.**

Am-plwah

Employer	Employeur
My **employer** is very nice.	Mon **employeur** est très gentil.

Am-plwah-yur

Employee	Employé

| I am an **employee** of this shop. | Je un **employé** de ce magasin. |

Am-plwah-yé

| Permanent position | Emploi permanent |
| I would like a **permanent position.** | J'aimerai un **emploi permanent.** |

Am-plwa pehr-mah-naan

| Temporary job | Emploi temporaire |
| I have a **temporary job.** | J'ai un **emploi temporaire.** |

Trah-bah-joh-tem-po-rahl

| Salary | Salaire |
| I want a **salary** increase. | Je veux une augmentation de **salaire.** |

First and last name are very common expressions, and so far, you must have used it a dozen times. However, we will need it to write your CV, so just in case…

| First name | Prénom |

| What is your **first name**? | Quel est votre **prénom**? |

Pré-nom

| Last name | Nom de famille |
| My **last name** is Dubois. | Mon **nom de famille** est Dubois. |

As you can surely guess, "nom de famille" means "family name".

Nom-duh-fa-mee

| Profession | Profession |
| What is your **profession**? | Quelle est votre **profession**? |

Pro-phé-ssion

| Credentials | Justificatifs |
| Here are my **credentials**. | Voici mes **justificatifs.** |

Ju-stee-fee-cah-teef

| Skills | Compétences |

| These are my main **skills**. | Voici mes **compétences** principales. |

Com-pé-tan-suh

As we know, the job market is different from how it was years ago. For many companies around the world, degrees and qualifications are not as important as they used to be. Therefore, a complete list of your knowledge and skills is very important.

| Job title | Titre de poste |
| My **job title** is Manager. | Mon **titre de poste** est responsable. |

Tit-ruh duh pos-tuh

| Job description | Description de poste |
| That is not under my **job description.** | Cela n'est pas dans ma **description de poste.** |

Des-krip-see-on-the-post

Your job description is, of course, crucial. While your job title might say something, your job description should provide a specific idea of what is expected from you.

Milestone	Jalon
What is your favorite **milestone**?	Quel est ton **jalon** preferée?

Jah-lon

As we already said, where you worked in the past and for how long it doesn't matter anymore. What truly matters is what you have accomplished in the past. Choose wisely your greatest "jalon" to prove your skills.

Manager	Responsable
Congratulations! You are the new **manager**.	Felicitations! Vous êtes le nouveau **responsable**.

Rés-pon-sah-bluh

Congratulations! I am so happy for you!

That escalated quickly, huh?

You know my motto: practice makes perfect! Let's dive into our next dialogue.

Manager (responsable): *Hello! What can I do for you?*

	Bonjour! Que puis-je faire pour vous?
Owen:	*Hello! I am looking for employment.*
	Bonjour! Je recherche un emploi.
Manager	*What is your name?*
	Quel est votre nom?
Owen:	*Owen Miller.*
	Owen Miller.
Manager	*Very well. What type of work are you looking for?*
	Très bien. Quel type de travail recherchez-vous?
Owen:	*I would like anything. Even a temporary job.*
	J'aimerais n'importe lequel. Même un emploi temporaire.
Manager	*Right. Did you bring your CV?*
	D'accord. Avez-vous votre amené CV?
Owen:	*Yes. Here it is.*

	Oui. Le voici.
Manager	*Very good. What are your major skills?*
	Très bien? Quelles sont vos principales compétences?
Owen:	*I am good at logo design.*
	Je suis doué en conception de logo.
Manager	*What are your most relevant milestones from the past year?*
	Quels sont vos jalons les plus pertinents de l'année dernière?
Owen:	*I won campaigns for logo refreshments in 5 major companies.*
	J'ai gagné des campagnes pour l'élaboration de nouveaux logos dans 5 grandes entreprises.
Manager	*All right. We will call you for another interview.*
	D'accord. Nous vous appelerons pour un autre entretien.

Owen:	*Do you have any vacancies?*
	Vous avez des postes vacants?
Manager	*We have a job for a designer. It could turn into a permanent position.*
	Nous avons un projet pour un designer. Cela pourrait devenir un poste permanent.
Owen:	*That is great.*
	C'est super.
Manager	*Yes, it is. You would get entry salary plus bonuses.*
	Oui. Vous toucheriez un salaire de base, plus des bonus.
Owen:	*Awesome. I will wait for your call.*
	Genial. J'attends votre appel.

We already had a little walkthrough for an interview, but we will work harder on that in the next chapter. After all, we have to get you ready for your first big job.

Chapter 10 – Bring, Learn & Lead

As the title of this chapter suggests, now is the time to bring, learn and lead, because you have to shine in your job interview. This is the time to talk about your ambition, show how good you are at planning and projecting, and demonstrate why you will be a great fit. To do so, we will need to introduce a new tense: the future.

As you will see, the future is formed by the infinitive of the verb (and not the root) plus the termination of the future, which is the same for all the 3 conjugations. Amazing right?

First verb: "to bring" – "apporter". As you will see, we'll take the infinitive "apporter" and we all add the terminations:

Ah-por-té

To bring	Apporter	Infinitive	Termination
I will bring	J'apporterai	Apporter-	Add "ai"
You will bring	Tu apporteras		Add "as"

He/She/It will bring	Il/elle apportera		Add "a"
We will bring	Nous apperterons		Add "ons"
You will bring	Vous apporterez		Add "ez"
They will bring	Ils/elles apporteront		Add "ont"

The good thing is that a job interview comes down to talking mostly about yourself. Therefore, it is important to know all the conjugations before you talk about your plans for specific people or other departments. The main goal, however, is learning to talk about yourself.

J' ah-por-tuh-réh

Now, let's go through examples.

I will bring all my experience.	J'apporterai toute mon experience.

He will bring many resources.	Il apportera beaucoup de ressources.
We will bring a new selling strategy.	Nous apporterons une nouvelle stratégie de vente.
They will bring everything we need §for this project.	Ils apporteront tout ce dont nous avons besoin pour ce projet.

With verbs ending in -RE, things work the same way, but you just have to remember to drop the -E of the infinitive before adding the termination of the future.

For exemple, with the verb "aprendre", you remove the last -E

To learn	Apprendre	Infinitive (without -e)	Termination
I will learn	J'apprendrai	Aprendr-	Add "ai"
You will learn	Tu apprendras		Add "as"

He/She will learn	Il/elle apprendra		Add "a"
We will learn	Nous apprendrons		Add "ons"
You will learn	Vous apprendrez		Add "ez"
They will learn	Ils/Elles apprendront		Add "ont"

Again, let's take a moment to focus on you: ah-pren-dré.

I will learn in this company.	J'apprendrai au sein de cette compagnie.
He will learn from this experience.	Il apprendra de cette expérience.
We will learn through hard work.	Nous apprendrons en travaillant dur.
They will learn a lot.	Ils apprendront beaucoup.

From a hiring perspective, "to lead" is a very important verb. Being able to lead is a well-appreciated skill for most recruiters, especially for some positions.

To lead	Diriger	Infinitive	Termination
I will lead	Je dirigerai	Diriger-	Add "ai"
You will lead	Tu dirigeras		Add "as"
He/She will lead	Il/Elle dirigera		Add "a"
We will lead	Nous dirigerons		Add "ons"
You will lead	Vous dirigerez		Add "án"
They will lead	Ils/Elles dirigeront		Add "án"

Guh-dee-ree-guh-reh

You will lead this project.	Tu dirigeras ce projet.
She will lead this department.	Ella dirigera ce département.

| We will lead the first part of the conference. | Nous dirigerons la première partie de la conference. |
| They will lead us to success. | Ils nous dirigeront vers le succès. |

The next verb to look at is the verb "to be". It is with this verb that I first learned the auxiliary for the future (will) and its uses. More than that, it gives you a basic structure for putting sentences together in the "futur simple", the most commonly used tense for the future.

To be	**Ser**
I will be	Je serai
You will be	Tu seras
He/She will be	Elle sera
We will be	Nous serons
You will be	Vous serez
They will be	Ils seront

First, let's practice with the future tense of "être".

I will be the leader in this project.	Je serai le dirigeant de ce projet
He will be a great asset to this team.	Il sera un grand atout pour cette équipe
This software will be great for us.	Ce programme sera super pour nous.
They will take care of everything.	Ils se chargeront de tout.

You can see that for French, the words "will be" compress to form a simple idea: "je serai". This is the French form for "to be" that will happen in the future.

With this, you can create sentences talking about what you have planned for the future.

"With these changes, we will be the first company in our field."

"Avec ces changements, nous serons la première compagnie dans notre domaine."

Now, let's check our final verb, "Avoir". (be careful, it's irregular)

To have	Avoir
I will have	J'aurai
You will have	Tu auras
He/She will have	Il/Elle aura
We will have	Nous aurons
You will have	Vous aurez
They will have	Ils auront

Another form of future which is also used quite often is the "futur proche", the "near future".

As for the past(with the Passé recent), this is your life jacket whenever you want to talk about the future. This form of future requires the conjugation knowledge of only one verb, which will fit for all. Let's see how this works:

The « futur proche » is formed by the verb « Aller » - « to go » in the present, followed by a verb with the infinitive.

Here's the conjugation of « to go », in French :

To go	**Aller**
I go	Je vais
You go	Tu vas
He/She goes	Il/Elle va
We go	Nous allons
You go	Vous allez
They go	Ils vont

Let's practice with some examples :

Look, it is going to rain !	Regardes ! Il va pleuvoir
I am going to do some shopping.	Je vais faire quelques achats.
You are going to travel next week.	Tu vas voyager la semaine prochaine.
We are going to sleep now.	Nous allons dormir maintenant.

Yes. I can almost hear you talking. No worries. We will see more of these examples in the next dialogue.

Mr. King:	*Hello. Are you Leo Mitchell?*
	Bonjour, êtes-vous Leo Mitchell?
Leo:	*Good afternoon. Yes, I am.*
	Bonjour. Oui, c'est moi.
Mr. King:	*Perfect. Please, come with me.*
	Parfait. Venez avec moi, s'il-vous-plaît.
Leo:	*Sure.*
	D'accord.
Mr. King:	*Tell me, Leo. If we hire you, what will you bring to the company?*
	Dites-moi, Leo. Si on vous embauche, qu'est-ce-que vous apporterez à l'entreprise?
Leo:	*I will bring 10-year experience in conflict and risks management.*

	J'apporterai 10 ans d'experience en management de conflits et risques.
Mr. King:	According to your knowledge, when will the updates be made?
	Selon votre expérience, quand pourrez-vous mettre en place les changements?
Leo:	I will have updates done within the first semester of 2020.
	Je les mettrai en place le premier semestre de 2020.
Mr. King:	What will you need to achieve that?
	De quoi aurez-vous besoin pour y parvenir?
Leo:	I will need a team, including two technicians.
	J'aurais besoin d'une équipe, incluant deux techniciens.
Mr. King	Very well. When can you start?
	Très bien. Quand pouvez-vous commencer?
Leo:	Next week works for me.

La semaine prochaine me va bien.

Mr. King Great. I am going to arrange an office for you.

Super. Je vais m'organiser pour vous trouver un bureau.

Leo: Thank you very much. And I am going to prepare for my first day as much as I can.

Merci beaucoup. Et moi je vais me préparer pour mon premier jour autant que possible.

I hope you are cracking this. All languages are about structure and, even if some are more complex than others, they become natural with time and practice. By the way, have you had a look at your new office?

Chapter 11 – New Job, New Life

I always feel a bit uncomfortable the first time I am in a new place, especially if it is going to be my new work environment! Of course, I also think it's great to meet new people, build friendships and more generally have the chance to network with other peers.

You won't have to worry as we are here to prepare you for what is coming. Do you want to join me?

Please, join me in your new office.

Office	Bureau
This is your **office.**	Voici votre **bureau.**

Bu-ro

Computer	Ordinateur
Your **computer** is ready to use.	Votre **ordinateur** est prêt à être utilisé.

Database	Base de données

www.LearnLikeNatives.com

| I granted you access to this **database**. | Je vous ai donné l'accès à cette **base de données.** |

Bah-se-the-do-né

Software	Programme
We have the best **software** to manage our database.	Nous avons le meilleur **programme** pour gérer notre base de données.

Pro-gra-muh

Keyboard	Clavier
This is a nice **keyboard**.	Celui-ci est un bon **clavier**.

Kla-vee-eh

Monitor	Écran
I need a larger **monitor**.	J'ai besoin d'un **écran** plus grand.

Eh-kran

Mouse	Souris
My **mouse** is ergonomic.	Ma **souris** est ergonomique.

Soo-ree

Hard drive	Disque dur
That is a 2 terabyte **hard drive.**	C'est un **disque dur** de 2 terabytes.

This-cuh-duh-ruh

File	Dossier
You will find all you need in the **file.**	Vous trouverez tout ce dont vous avez besoin dans le **dossier.**

Fee-chee-eh

Document	Document
I already sent that **document.**	J'ai déja envoyé ce **document.**

Do-cu-men

Report	Rapport
I will send the **report** this afternoon.	J'enverrai le **rapport** cet après-midi.

Ra-por

Coordinate	Coordonner

We need to **coordinate** that meeting.	Nous devons **coordonner** cette reunion.

Ko-or-di-neh

Desk	Bureau
This is a nice **desk.**	C'est un joli **bureau.**

Bu-ro

In French, we use the same word to talk about an office and a desk.

Department	Departement
I work for the Human Resources **department.**	Je travaille pour le **departement** des Ressources humaines.

Dé-par-tuh-men

Coworker	Collègue (de travail)
I had lunch with a **coworker.**	J'ai déjeuné avec un **collègue.**

Ko-leh-guh

Are you eager to practice? Great! Let's do this!

Eli: *How do you like your new office?*

Tu aimes bien ton nouveau bureau?

Jace: *I like it a lot. I think I will need another monitor to split screens.*

J'aime beaucoup. Je pense que j'aurai besoin d'un autre écran.

Eli: *Most coworkers do. We can coordinate that with the IT Department.*

La plupart des collègues en ont deux. On peut coordonner ça avec le service technique.

Jace: *Perfect. Thank you. I love my desk.*

Parfait. Merci. J'adore mon bureau.

Eli: *Yes. We invest in computers, software, and great equipment.*

Oui. Nous investissons dans des ordinateurs, des logiciels et du bon équipement.

Jace: *When are you expecting to have the files you requested?*

Quand avez-vous besoin des dossiers que vous avez demandé?

Eli: *Tomorrow is fine.*

Demain, c'est bon.

Jace: *Good. I just have to add a few documents.*

D'accord. Je dois juste rajouter quelques documents.

Eli: *Great, Jace! I think you will be a great addition to our team.*

Génial, Jace! Je pense que tu sera un très bon attribut pour notre équipe.

Jace: *Thank you for trusting in me. I will not let you down*

Merci de me faire confiance. Je ne vous décevrai pas.

How was your first day on the job? Are you already familiar with the coffee machine? You'd better work hard as you are going to be very busy soon.

www.LearnLikeNatives.com

A Quick Message

A quick message before we start the final chapter of this book.

"No one can whistle a symphony. It takes a whole orchestra to play it." –

H.E. Luccock

Do you want to be part of the orchestra of the Learning French community?

Here is how:

If you're enjoying this book, I would like to kindly ask you to leave a brief review on Amazon.

Reviews aren't easy to come by, but they have a profound impact in supporting my work. This way, I can keep creating new content to help the whole community at my very best.

www.LearnLikeNatives.com

I would be incredibly thankful if you could just take a minute to leave a quick review on Amazon, even if it's just a sentence or two!

It's that simple!

Thank you so much for taking the time to leave a short review on Amazon.

The community and I are very appreciative, as your review makes a difference.

Now, let's get back to learning French!

Chapter 12 – Bringing Home the Bacon

You have been preparing for this moment. You got yourself a new job, you have a new office and work team, and now is the time to start closing some business and bringing home the money. As always, let's first go with the essentials.

Meeting	Réunion
We have everything ready for the **meeting.**	Tout est prêt pour la **reunion.**

Re-u-nion

Sell	Vendre
We plan to **sell** when it reaches $95.	Nous plannifions de **vendre** quand il atteint $95.

Ven-druh

Take your time to practice that final "r" sound.

Capital	Capital

| We need to raise **capital.** | Nous devons augmenter le **capital.** |

Ka-pi-tal

| Market | Marché |
| The **market** is shifting. | Le **marché** est en train de changer. |

Mar-sheh

| Stock market | Bourse |
| The **stock market** could crash. | La **bourse** pourrait s'éffondrer. |

Boor-suh

| Project | Projet |
| The new **project** is very complex. | Le nouveau **projet** est très complexe. |

Pro-jeh

| Budget | Budget |
| The available **budget** is 750k. | Le **budget** disponible est de 750 mille. |

www.LearnLikeNatives.com

Bud-jé

Presentation	Présentation
I'll have the **presentation** ready by 1 pm.	La **presentation** sera prête à 13h.

Pre-sen-ta-sion

Supply	Offre
The **supply** is decreasing for some commodities.	L'**offre** diminue pour certains produits.

Off-ruh

Demand	Demande
The people **demand** new solutions.	Les gens **demandent** de nouvelles solutions.

De-man-duh

Experience	Expérience
I have 7 years of professional **experience**.	J'ai 7 ans d'**expérience** professionnelle.

Ex-pe-riehn-suh

Invoice	Facture

| I will send you my **invoice**. | Je vous enverrai ma **facture.** |

Fact-u-ruh

| Credit | Crédit |
| They have great **credit**. | Ils ont un superbe **crédit**. |

Cré-di

Just like the English word, but you don't pronounce the "t".

| Loan | Emprunt |
| I will pay half of the **loan**. | Vous payerez la moitié de **l'emprunt.** |

Am-prun

| Taxes | Taxes |
| I have to calculate my **taxes**. | Je dois calculer mes **taxes**. |

Tax-uh

| Investment | Investissement |
| It is a great **investment**. | C'est un super **investissement.** |

www.LearnLikeNatives.com

Ein-ves-tis-uh-man

Spend	Dépenser
It is important to **spend** in quality.	C'est important de **dépenser** en qualité.

Dé-pan-sé

Save	Economiser
We can **save** up to 30%.	Nous pouvons **économiser** jusqu'à 30%.

E-ko-no-mi-zé

Lose	Perdre
Sometimes you need to **lose**.	Parfois, tu dois **perdre**.

Per-druh

Here we are. This is the final test. This chapter's practice is meant to gather general knowledge from the last three chapters. Are you ready to buckle? Don't be scared. You got this.

    Mr. Reed : *I am going to be clear. I want a company to protect my investment.*

| | Je vais être clair. Je veux une compagnie pour protéger mon investissement. |

| Mr. Evans: | *Perfect. I can offer you all my experience for that job.* |
| | Parfait. Je peux vous offrir toute mon expérience pour ce travail. |

| Mr. Reed: | *What will be your strategy?* |
| | Quelle sera votre stratégie? |

| Mr. Evans: | *You have good credit. I plan to use a loan and increase the supply.* |
| | Vous avez un bon crédit. Je compte utiliser un prêt et augmenter l'offre. |

| Mr. Reed: | *How will I save capital that way?* |
| | Comment je vais économiser du capital comme ça? |

| Mr. Evans: | *By covering for the demand, I expect a rise in the Stock Market.* |
| | En couvrant la demande. J'attends une hausse de la bourse. |

Mr. Reed: *That will not do it alone.*

Ça ne fera pas l'affaire.

Mr. Evans: *I know. That is why we have a strategy to increase our market share by 3%.*

Je sais. C'est pourquoi nous avons une stratégie pour augmenter notre part de marché de 3%.

Mr. Reed: *Very well. I expect that you will have a great presentation for my board meeting.*

Très bien. J'attends que vous fassiez une superbe presentation pour le conseil d'administration.

Mr. Evans: *You know I will. My budget projections do not lie.*

Vous savez bien que oui. Mes projections de budget ne mentent pas.

Mr. Reed: *All right. I expect your invoice, then.*

Très bien. J'attends votre facture alors.

Mr. Evans: *I will be sending it tomorrow.*

Je vous l'enverrai demain.

I would like to get your opinion. How was this chapter for you? And now ask yourself: how could you improve your knowledge? As I have been saying from the beginning, you will be able to learn the language by repeating all the lessons in this book. And practice is the only way to do it—repeat it all out will help a lot.

Conclusion

Congratulations on making it through to the end of this book! You now have all the tools you need to achieve your French goals.

This is no science. Of course, there is a method, but it is mostly practicing, repeating, and doing! So, go for it. If you find yourself feeling unsure about something, just come back and look it up, and we'll go through it together! Yet, I am sure you already know so much, even more than you realize!

Look at all the things we did: we learned how to plan a trip, we discussed how to act if you or your family get sick, reviewed how to move around the city, ask for directions, and we had a nice conversation about how to talk about the past and the future.

We also learned how to deal with business in French: we talked about how to present a CV and become an employee. Also, we went through some commercial and business French to help you make great deals if you find yourself covering a management position.

Do you realize all the new things you can communicate now? You now have more resources for survival and regular living in a completely new environment, and I want to give you a big pat on the back for coming this far.

You can find the rest of the books in the series, as well as a whole host of other resources, at **LearnLikeNatives.com**. Simply add the book to your library to take the next step in your language learning journey. If you are ever in need of new ideas or direction, refer to our 'Speak Like a Native' eBook, available to you for free at **LearnLikeNatives.com**, which clearly outlines practical steps you can take to continue learning any language you choose.

Nevertheless, did I mention we are not over yet?
Now the fun part begins: try to watch your favorite cartoons in French, or try with some famous TV series, of course with French subtitles (yes French subtitles, you can make it!). If you like french movies, why not watch a Louis de Funès movie? They're big classics and fun to follow, yet extremely helpful for improving your French!

Again, thank you for listening. I hope to meet you in the near future so we can learn even more!

www.LearnLikeNatives.com

www.LearnLikeNatives.com

Learn Like a Native is a revolutionary **language education brand** that is taking the linguistic world by storm. Forget boring grammar books that never get you anywhere, Learn Like a Native teaches you languages in a fast and fun way that actually works!

As an international, multichannel, language learning platform, we provide **books, audio guides and eBooks** so that you can acquire the knowledge you need, swiftly and easily.

Our **subject-based learning**, structured around real-world scenarios, builds your conversational muscle and ensures you learn the content most relevant to your requirements.
Discover our tools at *LearnLikeNatives.com*

When it comes to learning languages, we've got you covered!

www.ingramcontent.com/pod-product-compliance
Lightning Source LLC
Chambersburg PA
CBHW071728080526
44588CB00013B/1937